12596

All Out for Everest

All Out for Everest

MICHAEL MONTGOMERY

with verses by

JOHN ASKE

PAUL ELEK   LONDON

To our long-suffering companions,
especially Bruce

© 1975 Michael Montgomery

Published in Great Britain by
Elek Books Limited
54–58 Caledonian Road, London N1 9RN

ISBN 0 236 40012 6

Produced by computer-controlled phototypesetting,
using OCR input techniques, and printed offset by
UNWIN BROTHERS LIMITED
The Gresham Press, Old Woking, Surrey .

CONTENTS

LIST OF PLATES

The photographs were taken by the author

Maps

PROLOGUE

Battersea High Street, a converted stable-yard, mid-October, dusk. If it was not actually raining, it ought to have been.

'Adventure of a lifetime,' the ad in the Personal Column of *The Times* had read, 'four months overland trek to the Everest Base Camp—see the world's highest mountain for yourself!'

I had noticed it while I was filling in time with the crossword as I awaited my turn to bat on a windy, autumnal Sunday afternoon—the sort of afternoon when the leaves begin to fall in earnest. It could not have caught me at a more vulnerable moment: my first novel was at long last out of the way, I had recently resigned my job with a family company and the cricket season was all but over. My turn eventually came, but my mind was still somewhere deep in the Himalayas; not surprisingly I was soon on my way back again, ignominiously run out after failing to respond to my partner's call for a quick single.

To see Everest for myself . . . the ambition had first stirred in me during my early geography lessons and had revived from time to time, but now, over twenty years later, it was still no nearer realisation. A recent television programme on Chris Bonington's planned assault on the mountain's south-west face had all but killed it for good: when it came to dangling on the end of a rope above a sheer drop of several thousand feet or picking my way out of a crevasse with an ice-axe, I was clearly a non-starter. There was no mention of any of this in the ad, however. Could it be that it was only above Base Camp that it all happened?

It was time, I decided, to find out; if I left it much longer, the chance would be gone for ever.

The next morning I went down to the local library and flicked through Edmund Hillary's account of his ascent. He talked of 'a leisurely march to the foot of Everest in perfect weather, swimming in rivers, eating enormous meals, sleeping out under the stars'. That didn't sound particularly strenuous, no more so than the average cricket tour.

'Just a jolly hike,' the ex-army type responsible for the ad confirmed when I rang for further details. 'Not literally all the way, of course: we get you as far as Kathmandu in a Land-Rover, but after that you'll be on your own two pegs.'

'What would I need in the way of equipment?'

'A good, sound pair of boots first and foremost, sleeping bag, anorak and enough clothes to keep you warm, but apart from that everything else is laid on.'

'And how many other people are going?'

'Ten's the top whack; any more than that and we find that everybody gets on top of one another. Mind you, that can happen anyway when there are girls aboard.'

'Girls?'

'Yes, we've got three coming on this one so far. Afraid I can't tell you more about them at the moment except that two of them are nurses which should come in handy up in the mountains, but we've had one or two real eye-catchers in the past. In fact, we usually get a pretty good mixed bag—accountants, secretaries, lawyers, all those sort of people, doing their best to get out of the rat race.'

'Are you going yourself?'

'Wish I could, old man, but somebody's got to sit here dealing with all the bumf. The leader's done the trip twice before, so he knows the whole thing inside out. First-rate chap; you won't go far wrong in his hands.'

'So there's no element of danger about it, I take it.'

'Danger? Good Lord no. You might get a touch of gut trouble from time to time, especially if you take a fancy to melons which have been floated down the Kabul river, and you might come across the odd snake—one of the girls on the last trip went behind a bush for a you-know-what and came out again pretty sharp-ish—but if you keep your eyes open and use a bit of commonsense you won't come to any harm. So how do you like the sound of it?'

'Well, I'll have to think it over.'

'Of course, old man, you do that. But don't leave it too long—I've only got a couple of places left and it takes a bit of time fixing up visas, getting jabs and all that sort of thing. I'll pop all the

gen in the post for you, and if you've got any questions after that,
just give me a buzz. Be hearing from you. Cheerio.'

When it arrived, the promised brochure spoke of the joys of
camping beside mountain streams and of the Nepalese delicacies of
congealed yak blood drawn from the jugular vein and tea served
with lumps of rancid butter floating in it. I found such enthusiasm
not altogether infectious. However, a few days' headlines devoted
to the threatened miners' strike and prospect of a coal-less English
winter soon made up my mind for me. After all, what on earth was
the point in freezing to death on Harrow-on-the-Hill, four
hundred feet above sea-level, when I could be doing just that on
the side of Mount Everest?

That had been a month ago, a month mostly taken up
alternating between interminable queues at the visa sections of
various embassies and the vaccination department of the Hospital
for Tropical Diseases. It had taken almost as long to persuade any
of my family that I was actually in earnest; my task was not made
any easier by the fact that almost all of them seemed to have seen
the Bonington programme.

'Oh yes?' They would say in tones of polite and not-so-polite
disbelief. 'And what mountaineering have you ever done before?'

'Well, I went up Ben Arkle when I was in Scotland last year.'

'On a rope?'

'No, just walking and scrambling.'

'That's not going to get you very far up Everest, you know.'

'Far enough for my purposes: it's not as if I'm going to try to get
to the top.'

'Nor the bottom either, if you ask me.'

The general diagnosis put it down to a case of post-novel
depression; even if I started out, they reassured themselves, I
would come to my senses long before I ever set foot in the
Himalayas. One of my more facetious friends insisted in referring
to the 'Bonington-Montgomery Expedition'; another conjectured
that my real object was to follow the forthcoming MCC tour of
India and offered to lend me his binoculars for the purpose. They
were only finally convinced by the assembly of items with which
they had never previously associated me: anorak, tracksuit,
sleeping bag, air-bed, trekking boots, water bottle, a pair of kitbags,
anti-malaria tablets.

As the evening dies around them
The nine approach their assignation
With quickening footsteps.
From north, south and west they come
Already full of distance
And breathing the thin, sunlit air
Of imagined Himalayas.
The message has gone out
And they come—strangers
With living armour in their blood—
They come for reasons
They may never fully understand
And in the fading light, their shadows
Point like dark fingers
Eastward.

Now, at the moment of departure, Everest seemed if anything, rather more remote. The nine adventurers stood in a silent, apprehensive circle watching their kitbags being loaded into the Land-Rover's trailer and at the same time making the first furtive assessments of one another. The leader and his co-driver brought the total complement to eleven, and even in the dwindling light I was aware that my six-foot-three-inches was not going to make me anyone's favourite neighbour.

The ex-army type and his wife sat in the office preparing our rations for the first few days.

'I thought you said there wouldn't be more than ten of us at the most,' I protested.

'Well, yes, I may have done, but this other chap was frightfully keen to join and I didn't have the heart to put him off.'

'Do the rest of us get a refund, then?'

'No, sorry old man, that's out of the question: we work on tight enough margins as it is.'

'I can believe it,' I muttered, chastened by the sight of an enormous stack of cheese sandwiches. (It was only when we were safely across the Channel that it was divulged that yet another person was to join us in Delhi.)

I resumed my place in the circle.

Presently the balding figure beside me said: 'There's a pub just down the road. Let's go and oil the wheels, shall we?'

Thus John and I were introduced.

Between rapid pints of beer he recounted his life history: attendance at most (or so it seemed) of the universities of Europe, translator in several languages, tourist courier, stage manager, even, improbably, a ganger on a building site and now, still more improbably, the director of an import agency with a big line in Pakistani industrial scissors. In between all these diverse occupations he had dashed off several hundred poems.

'I write a bit too myself,' I managed to interpose at last.

'What, poetry?'

'No, I've just done a novel.'

'Your first?'

'Yes.'

'Oh.' His voice betrayed that mixture of apathy and apprehension which is everywhere reserved for the announcement of a first novel. 'Did you do anything before that?'

'No, not unless you count some articles for the *Investor's Chronicle* while I was working in the City.'

It was very evident that he didn't.

I was spared further humiliation from this polyglot Titan by the sudden arrival of an elfin figure dressed in jeans, anorak and tam-o-shanter; I had no difficulty in recognising her as another of my fellow-adventurers from the stable yard.

'Right pair of buggers you are,' she accused.

Those nearest to us at the bar gave us a strange look and began to edge towards the other end.

'I'm sorry,' I began, 'I'm not quite sure. . . .'

'Fancy you'd give me the slip, did you?'

'No, we just thought we'd have time for a pint, that's all.'

'One pint?' she retorted, eying our glasses which had been refilled only a minute earlier. 'Go on, you've been here all of twenty minutes; I could get milk out of a dead cow quicker than that.'

It occurred to me that the flush of her cheeks owed itself to something more than indignation. 'You wouldn't like to join us, would you?'

'I don't mind if I do, seeing as you're asking me,' she replied with mock hauteur. 'I'll have a whisky mac, please. The name's Heather but if you think I'm from Scotland, you're wrong. I'm Lancashire born and bred. That's not to say I haven't been working up there. I've been a District Nurse on Skye for the last couple of years, so if you fall off the top of the Cuillins or choke yourself on a haggis next time you're up there, you'll know who to expect. And if you want the vital statistics, I'm 28 and not yet married, but you needn't get the idea that that's why I'm here. Cheers.'

When we had had time to absorb this deluge of information, we introduced ourselves.

The whisky mac disappeared with impressive speed.

'I won't say that's my first of the day,' Heather admitted, 'but that's the only way they're going to get me aboard that bloody wagon. Daftest thing I've ever done in my life is signing up for this.'

'I'm beginning to agree with you,' I said with some feeling: it didn't sound as if I could rely on her to pull me through any altitude problems. 'You've never done this sort of thing before, then?'

'Are you kidding? The highest I've ever been is up Blackpool Tower and that made me sick as a cat. How about you two?'

'I once spent a fortnight on the Pennine Way,' John volunteered.

'Don't tell me you got any snow on your head there.'

'That was hardly the point of the exercise,' he replied with disdain, at the same time fingering the top of his skull. 'You can keep your mountains, they're all the same to me.'

'Then what the hell are you going all the way to bloody Everest for?' Heather demanded.

'I'm hoping to have a week's meditation at Thyangboche.'

'At where?'

'The Thyangboche monastery, half way up; it's one of the most important centres of Tibetan Buddhism.'

'Don't tell me you're one of them.'

'Buddhists? Yes, I am actually.'

'Go on.'

John evaded the challenge and asked the time. 'I never carry a watch myself,' he explained.

'Nearly seven,' I said, 'which is when we're meant to be back.'

'I suppose we'd better be getting along, then.'

'Yes.'

'Och, come on,' Heather expostulated, I'm not even half pissed yet.'

'And it's a fair old road ahead,' John added.

'All right, just one more,' I agreed.

A lantern-jawed young man met us at the door of the office; his very pale blue eyes contained little suggestion of welcome.

'You're John, Michael and Heather, I take it?'

'That's right.'

'Yes.'

'Ay.'

'I'm Fabian, your leader. Let's get one thing clear straight away: I intend to lead you lot from the front and not from behind, which means that when I give you a time, you all stick to it. Right?'

'Yes, I'm sorry,' John apologised, 'It was really my fault: I never carry a watch on principle.'

'It seems an odd sort of principle to me, but we won't go into that now. In the meantime we've got a ferry to catch, so I suggest you find yourself a spot in the Land-Rover.'

The rest of the party had already done so, and John and I were left to make what we could of the two rear corners—which was not very much, nor did our efforts to do so endear us any further with our companions.

After a few breezy words of farewell from the ex-army type, we were soon heading east along the Old Kent Road; only my discomfort persuaded me that something other than a weekend's golf at Sandwich or a fortnight on the Continent lay at the end of it.

The round of introductions was gradually completed as we emerged into the neon-bathed suburbs: June the other nurse, a SRN and of a more academic turn of mind 'Did you know that you have to boil water for twelve minutes to kill all known bacteria?'); Pam, a teacher at a Swiss school who claimed acquaintance with several of the Bonington expedition and produced large-scale maps of the Everest region as evidence; another John, the trainee co-driver and already well insulated against the prospect of cold by a luxuriant beard (this useful distinction for purposes of reference was later made redundant by John Aske's subsequent growth, and he became simply 'JC'); Malcolm, a journalist and easily identifiable as such by his sybaritic mien which marked him as a habitué of Fleet Street bars; Greg, an accountant from Adelaide, but who disclaimed any ability at cricket or any other association with his namesake from that city; Hugh, at eighteen the youngest of the party, whose apparent athleticism was a source of misgiving to its more elderly members; and Bruce, another journalist, who bore a striking facial resemblance to a well-known comedian. 'You're mocking me,' he obliged, 'now don't mock, you mustn't mock, really; it's cruel, you know, it really is. I mean, I'm only on the job, aren't I? Don't laugh, you are vulgar people really, so vulgar. Now where was I? Ah yes, the prologue. . . !'

1   EUROPE: HELLO AND GOODBYE

We sailed at midnight for Zeebrugge.

I had innocently assumed that the 'all-in' fare included the use of a bunk on the crossing. I was soon disabused, as I was to be of most subsequent expectations of comfort in the next four months.

I enquired at the purser's office in the hope of an unclaimed cabin and was referred to the chief steward. Five others had preceded me, but as there were nine bunks still vacant it seemed that I had little to worry about—until the Frenchman in front of me told the steward: '*Je demande une place pour quartre personnes, s'il vous plait.*'

'*Excusez,*' I was moved to interrupt, '*avez-vous dit quatre personnes?*'

'*Oui: il y a ma femme, sa mère et sa soeur.*'

'*Mais où. . . .*'

At that moment three large and unmistakably Gallic females hove into sight at the top of the stairs.

'*Gabriel, ici!*'

They made a formidable trio and more than a match, I decided, for my execrable French.

I retired to search the ship for a row of unoccupied seats long enough to take my supine form. At length I found one backing on the ladies' toilets. I was no nearer sleep, however, for on my immediate left a matronly Cockney voice droned and cackled on and on into the night, and at the end of it—or rather at four o'clock, the hour of disembarkation—remarked: 'Did yourself a bit of all right there, didn't you, luv?'

I muttered something to the general effect that it was a pity that the Luftwaffe hadn't done a better job.

Bleary and shivering, we headed into the Belgian mist for the

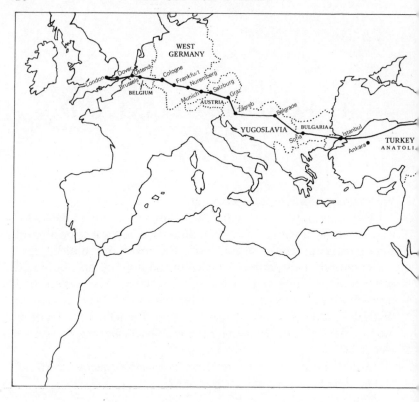

Route from London to Kathmandu

first of seven largely uneventful days that would take us across the breadth of Europe.

As soon as there was light enough to read by, Fabian circulated a list of jobs which he considered to fall outside his responsibilities as leader. He hoped that we could agree on their allocation among ourselves, but if not. . . .

Greg's application to administer the kitty was accepted without challenge; it was recognised that it would take a professional to make a sum of £75 a head to cover all our joint expenditure last out for four and a half months. The task of seeing that we each swallowed our daily dose of anti-malaria tablets clearly came as second nature to June, so that Heather was left with the role mistress of the medicine chest. Malcolm was a ready volunteer for

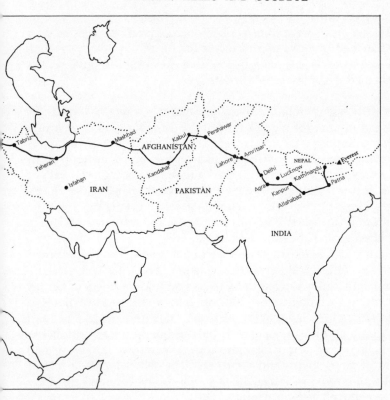

the post of 'equipment maintainer', doubtless in the hope that he would be able to discharge it from a sitting position, while John was no less slow to offer himself for that of 'route co-ordinator', which he understood to carry the onus of suggesting points of interest to be visited on the way (it soon became clear that this was not Fabian's interpretation of it). I found myself paired with Pam as a 'stores co-ordinator' for no better reason than that during my National Service I had once done a spell as mess food member; it did not turn out to be quite the sinecure that I had anticipated, for our first stock-taking revealed that we had set out from London without even such basic necessities as corned beef and detergent. Bruce took on the daily chore of packing and unpacking the trailer rather than be lumbered with that of filling the two 20-gallon jerrycans with water, which fell by default on poor Hugh.

All our meals were to be cooked on two paraffin stoves, and we were invited to make up our own pairs for the five-day rota. John did not conceal his indignation that he and I should be left unclaimed; I saw less cause for offence.

Our first night under canvas was spent in Cologne, which we reached in time for a quick tour of the cathedral and its environs. Being a Sunday, the streets were crowded with worthy burghers parading their heavy-jowled affluence, seemingly untroubled by the erection of a concrete car park not ten yards from the walls of what is arguably their country's finest monument to the Gothic ideal. The camp site was set a few miles out of the centre beside the Rhine and furnished with showers, a shop and restaurant. We were not often again to be similarly blessed.

John and I were issued with a tent and told to put it up; this we achieved after prolonged experiment. We unpacked our impedimenta and arranged them to our mutual satisfaction. On my side these included an air-bed; on John's, a horn, two flutes, a thermometer, microscope, telescope, tape-recorder, pipe and tobacco, a jar of malt, a pot of Hymettus honey, a set of fish hooks (as I discovered to my discomfiture), an extensive library, several pairs of Long Johns and a curious item of headgear—a sort of multi-coloured Balaclava helmet which he claimed to have emanated from the mountains of Peru.

Fabian came over to inspect our progress.

'Very nice,' he said in a tone which indicated that he was not quite as impressed as we had expected him to be, 'and where are the other two supposed to go?'

'The other two?' we repeated in horrified chorus.

'Yes—unless you're expecting six of us to share one of the others.'

'Well, no, . . .'

'And who said anything about bringing an air-bed?'

'I agree it wasn't on the list, but I assumed that was because it was so obvious.'

'It's funny that it didn't strike anybody else as being so obvious.'

'They can't have read their Hillary, then: I'm sure he said something about what a hell of a time he'd had blowing his up at Camp Nine.'

'When you get to Camp Nine, then I'll agree that you're entitled to one. In the meantime this is a four-man tent and that bloody thing takes up the space of two.'

'Well, one and a bit, perhaps.'

'All right, yours can be the bit that stays outside.'

'All right,' I agreed readily. It wasn't raining—then.

Even Fabian had to unbend when I came to inflate it: the foot-pump rose and fell with a rhythmic splutter until, reaching its climax, it gave off a noise which would have done credit to the rear end of a dyspeptic carthorse.

To emphasise his point, he himself moved into our tent together with the no more diminutive Hugh. Even lying head to tail (or more accurately, foot to mouth) still left half the air-bed projecting beyond the flap, so that when the rain did duly materialise, I had the choice of staying where I was and succumbing to it or of rolling off the bed and on to Fabian.

I chose the former.

Not surprisingly, dawn found me awake and ready for his savage tug on my leg, although still in no mood to stir. Five minutes later there was a sudden outrush of air and I sank gently to the ground. Reluctantly I acknowledged defeat.

Against John, who claimed the right to 'a few minutes yoga to set me up for the day', he adopted another and yet more drastic tactic: namely, that of dismantling the tent while he was still inside it.

Even this, however, was to prove not always effective.

At Frankfurt, the day's first stop, I made an important discovery among my companions: Bruce was a fellow-cricketer and equipped, moreover, with a tennis ball. The first game took place in the car park of a supermarket, much to the puzzlement of the attendant hausfraus; a length of board filched from an adjacent building site served for a bat. Lunch in a Bavarian forest yielded further refinements: a set of stumps and bails.

They proved valuable assets, as even the non-cricketers admitted: eight hundred miles of autobahn afforded few other sources of entertainment.

John, of course, excepted:

We are going to find the Yeti in his lair,
Yes, even if it takes us half the year.

And if he's big and hairy
We'll bring him back for Sister Mary—
We're going to find the Yeti in his lair.

We are going to seek the elephant and tiger,
Where the mountains are much higher than the Eiger
But if the tigers bite
We'll take immediate flight,
And go off to find the Yeti in his lair.

We are off to see the Yogi in his cell,
Where he blows his horn and rings his little bell,
But if the holy Yogi
Is a phoney or a fogey
We will leave the Yogi knotted in his cell.

We shall take the road that goes through old Kabul
Where ancient guns and turbans are the rule
But if we find a tribe are
Taking pot shots down the Khyber
We may stay a little while in old Kabul.

We may stay a little while in old Kabul
While the weather round about is growing cool
But since no one but a ghoul
Would spend Christmas in Kabul
Then we'll take the road out east of old Kabul.

Then we'll go to find a Yeti in his cave,
To share a chang with him and have a rave,
But if he's *really* scary
We'll bring him home for Sister Mary
Oh we're off to see the Yeti in his cave.

The mood of conviviality inside the Land-Rover grew in inverse proportion to the falling temperature outside as we approached the Alps, and after three days of each other's company we were strangers no longer.

The crush of bodies and the Land-Rover's uncompromising suspension ruled out any form of game (even dot cricket), and we resorted instead to an exchange of autobiographies. The two nurses regaled us with their fund of medical anecdotes, although June's attention to clinical detail was not to everyone's taste. It was soon found, however, that this tendency could be abruptly quelled by a prod at the more sensitive areas of her anatomy, which would reduce her to most un-SRN-like giggles. The culprit was usually Malcolm, whose features were daily made more lecherous by a darkening stubble; 'you won't catch me shaving in cold water,' he avowed defiantly—and superfluously. He had less luck with Heather: 'You keep your grubbies to yourself or I'll fetch you a bunch of fives,' she warned. It was probably more of a bluff than a threat, but it was said with sufficient force to deter him from putting it to the test.

Pam held herself aloof from these skirmishes, as if they detracted from the serious nature of the enterprise, and tried to divert us by tracing Bonington's likely route on her Everest map. She was seldom successful.

Divided from the rest of us with the two drivers in the front, Greg sat absorbed with sheets of figures; every time we crossed a border he became a bureau de change for everyone's petty cash. From time to time, however, he would throw out a pearl of Australianese; 'that rag wrings out like an Afghan's knickers,' he observed of the single washing-up cloth provided.

John's thermometer was already registering fifteen degrees of frost when we stopped for the night just short of the Schober Pass in eastern Austria.

'That's more like it,' Fabian said, and evidently meant it; we waited in vain for him to change from his tattered suit of jeans into something warmer.

Hugh's breath punctuated the darkness like squirts of aerosol spray as he humped the jerrycans back from a nearby stream.

'Nice to see the young working for a change,' Pam remarked in her best schoolmarm manner from the warmth of the Land-Rover, and indeed most of us were already guilty of exploiting his youthful physique and obliging nature. 'Leave it to Hugh, he'll fix it,' had become the cry whenever anything calling for some exertion was required to be done, such as driving tent pegs into the frozen ground. To his vast credit he accepted it all in good humour, demanding only in return a priority in the queue for second helpings. On this occasion, however, there were none, and he retired to his tent wearing the expression of, as Greg put it, 'a dingo with a sawn-off tit for a mother.'

The commissar who inspected our passports the next morning at the Yugoslav frontier might have come straight out of a cartoon: surly, bull-necked and bullet-headed. He summoned us each in turn to his plate-glass cabin to satisfy himself of some resemblance to our photographs.

John's lay at the bottom of the pile. The pudgy fingers flicked backwards and forwards through its pages several times before pushing it back to him unstamped.

'No.' It was said with relish.

'What?'

'No good.'

'Why not?'

'No.'

Unfortunately Serbo-Croat was not one of the several languages in which John claimed facility. He did what he could to indicate with his hands that the loss of his hair had been due to natural causes.

'No, no, no!' A great fist pounded the counter in emphasis.

John retreated to consider his next move.

Eventually an English-speaking official was found and the mystery explained: under a recent decree every British passport issued outside Britain required an affidavit to the effect that its owner was not an Asian displaced from Uganda, and John's had been issued in Paris. Wasn't this a matter of simple observation? Evidently not to the bureaucratic mind. He then recounted his impeccably Irish ancestry, but with no more success.

Various suggestions were made: couldn't he try just walking round behind the block? Couldn't we pack him into a kitbag? Couldn't he bury himself in one of the lorry loads of tomatoes waiting to cross? And others increasingly facetious.

There was nothing for it, Fabian decided, but to return to the nearest British Embassy—at Vienna, two hundred and fifty miles back.

We drove well into the night and stopped at a roadside *rasthaus*. John quickly drowned his remorse in a two-litre mug of the local brew and tottered off to bed. When I followed an hour later, however, there was no sign of him.

Reveille found him standing in front of the mirror, fingering a quite magnificent black eye.

'How in the hell did you get that?'

'Well, actually I'm not quite sure, to be perfectly honest. I went out for some fresh air and I think I must have got a bit lost. Then it started to rain, so I went into this sort of barn and stumbled over a couple knocking it off in the hay. I don't remember too much of what happened after that. . . .'

In the next moment, with a cry of agony, he did so: bending down to the basin, he struck the same eye on the tap which projected from the wall a foot or so above it.

The injury wrung no tears from Fabian, whose only concern was to get him to Vienna before the embassy opened. The rest of us were left behind to speculate on the effect that its appearance would have on the commissar.

I took myself and my camera off for the morning into the surrounding beech woods which were now at the peak of their autumnal brilliance. In the fields beyond, families of peasants were gathering the harvest of maize ripened to an orangeness which put to shame the pallid, pre-packed 'corn-on-the-cobs' familiar to the city-dweller. The stalks were also loaded on to a horse-drawn cart and taken off to a farmyard, where the elderly owner supervised his wife stacking them into a barn (the site of John's nocturnal encounter?). He was much flattered to be photographed, but equally puzzled that I should wish to include her. The scene epitomised the timelessness of the rural round; Breughel would have recognised it; even, perhaps, Vergil.

The Land-Rover presently returned, mission completed, and we set out again for Yugoslavia.

We were greeted again by the same unsmiling features; each passport was subjected to the same intense scrutiny. John's was again the last. The porcine eyes fixed themselves balefully on his disfigurement, until he felt moved to an explanation. His attempt to indicate in a sign language just how absurd a position it was that the Austrians were in the habit of putting their taps became necessarily somewhat involved, and even the commissar was seen to wilt. Suddenly he held up a hand to concede defeat, and with the other banged a stamp down on the passport.

We were through.

The 'autoput' proved truly a motorway of the people, running four hundred miles across the already undistinguished Serbian plain. Even at its widest it could barely accommodate two abreast of the titanic, windscreen-filling lorries that charged along it undeterred by the frequent carcases of ill-starred predecessors. We were thankful to exchange it at Nis for the secondary road which led to Bulgaria.

It was the turn of John and I to produce the evening meal. A budget of ten pence a head seemed to preclude anything very ambitious, but John had other ideas:

'I think a Boeuf Stroganoff would go down rather well, don't you?'

'I'm sure it would, if we could afford it.'

'Oh, it won't cost much: four pounds of steak should be enough, and after that we only need a few onions, peppers, rice, cream, cooking wine, bay leaves. . . .'

I could see that nothing I said was going to deter him.

He met his match, however, in the 'supermarket': instead of steak it offered only thin slices of frozen cod, instead of rice only small, shrunken potatoes, instead of wine only slivovitch, and even John confessed himself uncertain of the latter's culinary properties. A glance at a newspaper kiosk indicated that in other matters the country was more alive to the tastes of the decadent West, although the lovely ladies on the magazine covers displayed somewhat more hair than would perhaps be considered attractive there.

It began to rain. We fell in behind a bedraggled wedding procession making its way slowly up the moist street. The bride danced bravely on to the detriment of her white dress; a flautist and a double-bass provided original, if discordant accompaniment.

The terrain now took on a wilder aspect as we climbed towards a range of mountains which marked the border. It was dark before we levelled out again; finding a suitable spot for the night was clearly going to be something of a problem. After several abortive stops, Fabian turned off down a narrow track. We bumped over a level crossing, then suddenly one of the front wheels sank up to its axle into soft earth, giving the whole vehicle an alarming list to port. The order to abandon was given; all we could do until the morning was to make it fast to a tree on the other side and pray that the rope would hold.

Pitching tents in the mud and the rain was difficult enough, but for the cooks, deprived of the use of the headlights, the disaster was total: I mistook the salt for the sugar, John confused the flour with the powdered milk, I peeled my fingers rather better than I did the potatoes, John tripped on a guy rope and shot the cauliflower into the middle of a blackberry bush, someone else kicked over the kettle just as it boiled. Our ancient primuses, temperamental at the best of times, made it only too clear that they could not be expected to function under these conditions and when, finally, the meal was served, the cod was found to be so full of bones that most preferred to go hungry rather than risk death by choking. Nor did John's lyrical description of the last Boeuf Stroganoff that he had cooked himself in Hampstead bring much consolation.

Daybreak revealed the Land-Rover still poised at the same angle. Our best chance of extricating it, we decided, lay in digging away the embankment and replacing it with more substantial material, and to this end an impressive pile of boulders and branches was scavenged from the adjacent fields and riverbank. A splendidly moustachioed old man arrived to graze his horse and immediately took charge of the operation. Later spectators included a postman and two policemen; the latter presently withdrew in high dudgeon, their orders either ignored or countermanded.

When everyone was at last satisfied that it was safe to put the construction to the test the horse was recalled from its meal and harnessed to the front bumper. Deciding that there was little that I could contribute, I retired to the river for a quick bathe. Its waters, swollen and discoloured, were far from inviting, but they still made a refreshing change from clothes worn continuously now for a week. I returned to find the Land-Rover securely back on the road. We thanked the old man with a bottle of slivovitch, and he in turn insisted on shaking each of us by the hand before he would allow us on our way.

The Bulgarians showed themselves better pleased to see us than had their Yugoslav counterparts, but with better reason: they charged us four dollars a head for temporary visas. For this sum we received a brochure carrying the best wishes of the Committee for Tourism at the Council of Ministers of the People's Republic of Bulgaria and containing such ambivalent information as 'free road aid is rendered to motorists whose cars have suffered damages from the yellow cars of the Bulgarian Automobile Club'.

'Customs Formalities: no filling out of written declarations when entering the country,' it went on to proclaim. 'An oral statement of the valuables and securities carried will do.' It sounded too good to be true, and it was—not because of any false promise, it was simply that a bus load of Americans had beaten us to the one English-speaking official qualified to receive our statements of valuables (not to mention securities).

There was half an hour of daylight left when we were finally cleared; Istanbul, where we were booked into a hotel the following night, was still over four hundred miles away. Fabian offered us two alternatives: we could either go on another hundred miles to the camp site in Sofia or stop at a nice little spot he knew of just up the road. In vain did John and I point out the absurdity of doing fifty miles one day and four hundred the next, quite apart from the awful consequences hinted at in the brochure of being caught camping on an unauthorised site; the majority, it seemed, were concerned only to minimise the interval to the next meal.

The 'nice little spot' turned out to be a clearing in a young plantation; the trees afforded scant protection against the rigours to be expected at an altitude of six thousand feet.

We were once again lulled to sleep by the patter of rain on the canvas, although later it seemed to ease.

We woke up under six inches of snow.

Blinking in the unaccustomed glare, it took me a little time to realise that the other four-man tent was no longer where I had last seen it, and then that its occupants were huddled together inside the Land-Rover. Through chattering teeth (it was some hours before Malcolm fully recovered the power of speech) the tragedy gradually unfolded: what had begun as a leak had developed into a torrent until they had found themselves lying in several inches of water; then, just when they had succeeded against all the odds in baling it out, the whole tent had collapsed under the weight of the snow and now lay buried from sight. So much for democracy.

By the time that our numbed fingers had dismantled the tents, fumbled unsuccessfully to squeeze their much-increased bulk into their bags and eventually pummelled them into a size and shape that the trailer would accommodate, everyone was prepared to forgo breakfast for the relative warmth of the Land-Rover. The relief was short-lived, however, for eleven shivering bodies and eleven pairs of stamping feet soon created an even more uncomfortable condensation; it got so bad that books began to fall apart at the turn of a page.

By Sofia the snow had given way to a heavy mist; our only impression of the capital was of slush-puddled streets, deserted except for a few figures crouched in dim doorways.

By Plovdiv, a hundred miles further on, a wan sunshine was filtering through, although it brought no perceptible increase in the temperature and served merely to aggravate the condensation. We stopped to sample the delights of a State Restaurant: gruel and, just when we had despaired of their arrival, omelettes. In the main square hundreds of track-suited students were strolling about indifferent to the martial music blaring from loudspeakers. Above them a thirty-foot, cardboard Stakhanovite stared vacuously, a tractor wheel clasped in his bloodless hands.

Another hundred miles and we had left the country, rather less than twenty-four hours after entering it.

No one was heard to express any desire to return.

2 ISTANBUL: A WELCOME INTERLUDE

We reached Istanbul just before midnight.

The occasion was something less than magical: the city of Constantine, seat of the Roman and Ottoman Empires and still romanticised as the meeting-place of East and West, announced itself to us in the garish blaze of bank advertisements. *Turkiye is bankasi,* one of them proclaimed; it seemed no idle threat.

By now, however, after eighteen hours on the road, we were unappreciative of anything except the prospect of a bed and a roof above it which awaited us at the Hoteli Ayia Sofia.

'You're not staying *there,* are you?' John's friends asked in horror when he rang them the next day.

'Well yes, we are, actually. It's not too bad really.'

And in fact it compared quite favourably with a tent, even if we were sleeping four to a room. Its most interesting feature was the plumbing in the bathroom—or rather, the lack of it, for the waste was carried away along channels in the floor to a hole in the wall. It was not a strikingly efficient system: anyone attempting a bath had to approach it through three inches of stagnant water, and even those brave spirits quailed at the consequences of taking out the plug.

'But the other people. . . .'

They had a point: it was our first encounter with the hippy tribe who were now to mark our route all the way to Kathmandu. The neglect of their appearance was quite as conformist as the conventionality which they affected to reject, but more sobering still was the level of their conversation. The following was by no means an untypical example:

'Grass is real shit in Nepal.'

'Where's that, man?'

'You know, India, sort of.'

'Yeah?'

'Yeah. Real shit it was, and expensive. Jesus, it cleaned us right out of bread.'

'So you had a rip off?'

'Sure. There was this farmer guy, see, we moved in with and sussed his pad out; found a whole stack of corns, so we loaded them up and shifted them at the next town for bread. Must have been his whole crop, I reckon.'

This was received as something of a joke.

The Ayia Sofia could claim one advantage, however; as its name implied, it lay in the heart of the old city and so within easy range of the main points of interest.

We had hardly set foot from it before we were besieged by a horde of small boys pressing on us maps, guidebooks, postcards, trinkets, knives, even chips of marble.

I asked the price of a guidebook from an impish ten-year-old.

'Fifty lira.'

'Forget it, then.'

'What is your price?'

'Ten.'

He clapped a grubby hand over a smirk of mock hilarity.

'Thirty.'

'Still too much.'

'For you, last price twenty-five.'

'Fifteen.'

'Seventeen.'

'Sixteen.'

'All right, sixteen.'

'You very hard man.'

His expression of disappointment dissolved into delight as he pocketed the coins.

We went first to the Topkapi Palace. According to my purchase, it 'withholds one of the richest treasures on earth', and later I read elsewhere that its sale would solve the country's balance of payments problem overnight. Certainly the vast collection of Chinese porcelain (how did it survive all those thousands of miles on the back of a mule?) and model palace in solid gold from the same country, the statuette in black pearl from India and the dagger topped with three plum-sized emeralds from Persia—to mention only some of the more remarkable items—illustrated as nothing else could the former influence and extent of the Ottoman Empire.

Another milling crowd followed us to the Blue Mosque and its larger, older sister, the Santa Sofia, where one of the official guides laid about them enthusiastically with his umbrella. It was not to be the only occasion on which we witnessed the Turks' sadistic streak. Once he had dispatched the last of them to a respectful distance he became urbanity itself, astonishing us with an intimate knowledge of Nottingham Castle until, carried away by his success, he described Constantine (born in 280) as being the grandson of Hadrian (died in 138). Not even his loquacity, however, could quite gloss over a sense of disappointment with his subjects: apart from the Blue Mosque's ceramic tiles which gave it its name and the Santa Sofia's early Byzantine mosaics, their interiors had little to offer except rows of carpets worn bare by the countless genuflections of faithful knees.

As we explored further, however, we soon came to appreciate that the city's charm and curiosity lay in its people rather than its architecture—or, more accurately, in its menfolk, for although the veil has gone, the women have still not quite thrown off with it the tradition of self-effacement; in the ubiquitous small boys; in the taxi-drivers insistent to the point of importunity on the advantages of their aged American machines; in the proprietors of bookshops who, unable to offer anything in English, could still say with passionate sincerity 'it is lovely to have met you'; in the street-traders whose wares included everything from balloons to screwdrivers, from clockwork dolls to shaving brushes, with the hire of their bathroom scales as a sideline. Even those who had nothing to sell were no less ready to converse, direct, advise, instruct.

> I have seen autumn change to winter
> And cities shuffled like diamonds
> From a hand of days
> But here we rest.
> In the old city, it is quiet
> In the shadow of the great mosques
> And where the church of Saint Sofia
> Sleeps in her giant darkness

Like a sphinx.
From the roof, the Bosphorus
Spreads like a black mantle
Bordered with the lamps
Of streets and palaces, mosques,
Bazaars and riverboats, and from
The hurrying darkness in between
Pours a vigorous tide of humanity.
Tall and short, dark and fair,
The crooked and the straight,
All impelled by the inscrutable
Destiny of the evening.
Even in the new city, beyond
The tower of the Genoese,
The coloured lights do not remove
The air of secret purpose;
Somewhere for the seeker, there is
The wine of visionary sleep,
The nymph of all desire—
And surely, in this timeless city
Full of the wraiths of crowned byzantines
And imperious sultans—the one
Who walks silently, disguised by power,
The one who holds the hearts of men
Between his fingers, and to whom
Wisdom and folly are the same.
For a moment, he stands at the edge
Of eyesight, gleaming like a scimitar
In the dimness of an archway,
Then turns and vanishes
Like light through a closing door.

Returning to the hotel for a bath before dinner, I was again cut off by the same three inches of stagnant water. An appeal to the reception desk brought no more than a shrug of the shoulders and directions to the nearest Turkish baths. It seemed a drastic remedy, until I remembered the alluvium that still encrusted my person as a result of my dip in the river. Not being in quite such need himself, John declined to accompany me.

The directions proved far from precise, and I passed in and out of the offices of a leading newspaper before I traced my goal's rather scruffy facade to a dim side-street. Inside, however, lay a different world—a world of light and luxury, of gleaming marble, polished pine, fragrant perfume and delicious warmth.

The proprietor greeted me with a long list of all the refinements available, although he insisted that 'for you, Effendi, the full service is the best: it will make you the new man, I swear to you.'

I forbore to point out that his own figure, which verged on the obese, did little to lend credibility to this assertion.

'Thanks, but I think I'm capable of washing myself.'

'No, no, it is not possible for you: after the massage you must have the washing by the attendant.'

'Five lira seems rather a lot just for that.'

He looked at me with a mixture of pity and contempt.

'You are saying that five lira is too much for you? Where do you stay—the Hoteli Hilton?'

'No, not in fact.'

'Where then? Tell me.'

I hesitated, trying to assess what impact the Ayia Sofia would have on him.

'Ah, I understand,' he continued, winking pendulously. 'You stay with the woman, yes? She will love you much more after the washing, I swear to you, Effendi. I understand very well the women. She will love much better your skin, your smell—'

It was time, I felt, to put a close to the conversation. 'All right, I'll have the full service.'

'You are a very wise man, Effendi. That will be twenty-five lira altogether.'

A loin-clothed masseur was summoned to see me to my allotted cabin. Although clearly past the first flush of youth, his body was still disconcertingly muscular. As I changed into my own length of towelling I could see his feet standing guard outside, as if to dissuade me from any sudden impulse to make a run for it.

He led me through two oak doors sprung by massive stone weights suspended on ropes into the caldarium. For a minute or two I was aware of nothing except a swirling cloud of steam and the sound of water dripping and splashing; then gradually I made out a number of inert bodies being rolled about on a central platform like so many carcasses, and beyond them others seated around the walls, being sluiced down from taps set in the marble beside them.

1   Drivers pause for thought in Yugoslavia

2   Poet's corner at Eyup

3　Bruce on a Turkish wicket

4　John and the two footballers

'You go there,' he instructed, pointing to an alcove on the far side. 'I come back for you in one half of an hour.'

It was the hottest part of the room, being also the driest, and those already there looked to be in the last stages of dehydration. The novices among them were easily distinguished by their nervous reaction to every grunt and groan issuing from the mist, whereas the initiates merely smiled at each other in pleasurable anticipation.

Just when it seemed that I had no more sweat to offer, my would-be tormentor reappeared and beckoned me towards the platform. I lay face down and awaited the worst. He began gently enough with a finger lock, although even this produced an ominous crackling, and followed up with a kneading, slapping and pummelling over every inch of my body. Innocent that I was, I took this to constitute the main assault. It was to prove the merest skirmish. As I congratulated myself on my survival, he suddenly launched himself again on me. This time he tugged and twisted my arms almost from their sockets, bent my legs back to an angle usually associated with trussed chickens and twisted my head from side to side until I could feel the sweat from his armpits running into my ear. In a final show of victory—as if any were needed—he walked along my spine and performed a short dance on the small of my back.

'Okay?' He enquired routinely, jerking me to my feet.

I managed a nod.

'We go for the washing now.'

'Anything you say.'

I limped after him and lowered myself gingerly on to the marble slab indicated. After a vigorous shampoo he began on my shoulders with a bar of camphorated soap. When the time came to remove my loin-cloth he showed a surprising delicacy, averting his eyes rather as the sons of Noah did when, discovering him naked in his tent after overdoing the celebration of their deliverance from the Flood, they went backwards and put a rug over him. (If my familiarity with such an obscure passage of the Old Testament surprises, let me explain: towards the end of a term in my last year at prep school I had the bad luck to lose my Lesson Reader's card, and rather than own up I tried to work out my next lesson from those of my two fellow readers. Unfortunately the gap spanned a couple of chapters, and I chose the wrong one: as the headmaster somewhat curtly informed me afterwards in his study, I should have been describing the Miracle of the Rainbow. It was the last lesson that I ever read.) He rinsed the suds off and rubbed me over with a coarse-fibred glove, removing several layers of skin in the process.

He then delivered his final, knock-out blow: a basinful of icy water.

'Okay, it is finished now.'

Slowly, very slowly, I realised that the ordeal was over. It was all I could do to persuade myself to stay long enough to exchange my loin-cloth again for my clothes before making my escape.

The proprietor gave me another meaning wink as he saw me out into the street. I came away feeling very far from the new man that he had promised, but secure at least in the knowledge that I was now purged of Balkan silt.

'I'm going up to Pierre Loti's villa.' John announced in the morning, 'want to come with me?'

'That's another friend of yours, is it?'

'He just happens to have been one of the leading nineteenth-century French poets. He died at least sixty years ago.'

'Oh.'

'He also wrote a rather famous novel about Istanbul called *Aziyade.* You've read it, have you?'

'No, I must admit . . . . Where exactly is it?'

'His villa? It's on a hill at the far end of the Golden Horn. You might enjoy the ferry ride, if nothing else.' It was not the last time that he was to express disappointment in me.

'Yes, all right, I'll come.'

We traced the terminal to a quay on the far side of the Galata Bridge. Finding that we had forty minutes to spare before the next ferry, we climbed up to have a look at the tower of the same name from which, we learnt from the guidebook, 'in 17th Century was made the first successful recorded flight of man and the first intercontinental flight in the world. Hezarfen Ahmet Celebi flew from the top 2km. as far as to Uskadar across the Bosphorus with the hand-made wings attached to his arms'. By the same token, the seige of Constantinople in 1453 presumably saw the first exchange of intercontinental ballistic missiles.

Back at the quay, a row of men stood almost shoulder to

shoulder dangling lengths of nylon into the dun, oily water; the rails of boats moored alongside were also similarly occupied. The intensity of concentration shown would have won the grudging respect of any Thames-side club angler. Theirs was no mere pastime, however, for this seemingly unpromising source yielded a non-stop supply of sprats. Some were carted off in crates to a lingering death in the nearby fish market 'while others, more fortunate perhaps, were dropped into pans of boiling fat, fried for a minute or two over charcoal stoves and shovelled into cornets of newspaper—much to the chagrin of a motley of waiting cats, whose only spoils were the heads and bones discarded by the few more squeamish customers. The arrival of the ferry brought serious interruption of business, especially for those who were too slow to pull up their lines and found them entangled by its wash. We left two of the older men fighting it out over a knot of nylon and a single flailing fish.

The skyline's minarets presently gave way to dockyard cranes as we chugged upstream under a plume of dense, black smoke. A small boy sitting opposite on the open deck studied us intently as we conversed, then took a book from his satchel and with obvious pride opened it for our inspection. It was an English primer.

'This is a desk.' the first sentence stated firmly, under an appropriate illustration.

'This is a desk,' our companion announced haltingly, and looked up at us with large, soulful eyes for approval.

We nodded.

'This is a book,' he continued.

We nodded again.

'This is a pen, and this . . . .'

Evidently education in Turkey was still uninfected by 'discovery' methods.

'This is my home,' he said as we drew in beside a short, rickety pier. 'Farewell.' He shook us gravely by the hand and alighted.

We were put ashore at Eyup, 'holiest of holies, depository of the relics of the Prophet and the mortal remains of all the greatest believers, including those of his standard bearer, Eyup Ensari, for whom Mahomet II the Conqueror constructed a mosque and mausoleum.' The information was largely wasted on us, for by now the shrines of Islam had begun to assume very much of a muchness.

Passing a school, we were caught up in a stream of children emerging for their lunch hour. The girls seemed conscious of the effect of their black pinafores, which was to accentuate the darkness of their complexions and the lumpiness of their figures, and hung back a little; the boys, incongruously attired in Eton collars and jackets, were less inhibited.

'You speak English?' they demanded.

'Yes.'

'I speak English.'

'Good for you.'

'I am a student.'

'You have a desk?'

'Yes, yes.'

'You are a pen?'

'Yes, yes.'

We took refuge eventually in a café and ordered a meal from a menu which included Norwegian Brick, Meals in Oil, grilled Squared Meat and Beans Gigantes. Our pursuers pressed their noses against the plate glass to watch us eat until driven off by a furious proprietor wielding a clutch of kebab skewers. He was an imposing figure, with a bald head and a waxed moustache that recalled Eric Campbell, the eye-rolling giant of the early Chaplin films. He served us in person with our thimblefuls of coffee and sat down at the table.

'You German?'

We denied the accusation.

'Russian?'

Again we assured him otherwise. It was just as well.

'Russian I no like.' He illustrated the strength of this sentiment by drawing a finger across his throat, then stabbing it into his stomach with a motion which suggested a particularly gruesome disembowelment. I began to appreciate the value of his country's membership to the NATO alliance.

'We're English.'

'Ha. Englishmen is good.'

The ends of his moustache curled upwards into a circle of a smile, and with a crunching handshake he took his leave and returned behind the bar.

We set out for the poet's villa. The narrow, cobbled road led steeply uphill, causing us to pause for breath at the gates of a cemetery. There was nothing to indicate that access to it was barred to the infidel. We entered, and were soon swallowed up in a seething jumble of grass and stone, bramble and marble, bindweed and ironwork. The guidebook was, for once, accurate in its description of the headstones as 'ruinous': those that had not yet fallen to the ground leant at angles which threatened imminent destruction to anyone rash enough to pass within their range. Few of the graves except those granted the protection of railings were free of encroachment; some were fighting an unequal battle against burgeoning fig trees and similarly thrustful invaders; many had long since merged into their neighbours and in some cases looked as if they had simply been superimposed on each other. One, marked only by a humble, rusty plaque bearing the number 8822, had suffered particularly grievous neglect: an animal had burrowed within but had soon abandoned its loot, for the bones lay scattered about outside.

Presently we emerged into a small clearing whose occupants were now altogether without trace. John announced that his Muse was upon him and sat down on the corner of a tombstone, having first satisfied himself of its security. I found a more comfortable position against the trunk of a cypress and watched the excited puffs of smoke from his pipe rise into the cloudless sky. After a while they dwindled and died, but he wrote on, oblivious.

> On the hill, the dead lie
> Wrapped in the brown silence
> Of the earth—life
> Is a distant murmur.
>
> The sunlight is mingled
> With the voices of birds
> And the sudden brilliant flicker
> Of a butterfly.
>
> Around the graves, small yellow flowers
> Grow in profusion, summoning their light
> And colour from the rich clay
> Beneath them, while at my feet
> A tireless ant conveys its dead to earth.

As I sit watching silently, a lone bee
Crawls across the blank page of my notebook
And finding no honey, moves away
Among the names of the forgotten sleepers.

His shadow woke me. He held out a sheet of paper.

'What do you think of it?'

I blinked. John writes left-handed and at an angle of approaching 180° to the paper; to anyone else, and not infrequently to himself, the result is totally indecipherable.

After what I judged to be a suitable pause, I replied: 'Oh yes, I like that.'

'Good. I thought you would. Do you think we ought to be getting back?'

In the distance the waters of the Golden Horn were now appropriately gilded by the evening sun.

'Yes.'

We never did get to Loti's villa.

3   ASIA: A DAMP INTRODUCTION

We left Istanbul as we had entered it—on a note of disenchantment. My picture of the Bosphorus had been painted for me by the Greek Unseen in my Oxford Finals: a passage from Strabo (I think) describing the ferocity of the currents and the consequent variety of fish to be found there (at least, that had been my interpretation of it). As it was, cloud hung low and grey over it, while the continuous succession of the commuter ferries churning across its waters banished all visions of life beneath them. The skeleton of the new suspension bridge rising further upstream no longer seemed the blasphemy that it might have once. Nor when we reached the other side did we meet with the dramatic change that the division of the continents might have led us to expect; on the contrary, the coastline as far as Izmit seemed little more than a string of oil refineries, and the bank advertisements grew, if anything, still more numerous.

As we turned inland from the Sea of Marmora, the cloud unleashed its rain. It pursued us almost without break to Trebizond, a journey of four days—two in the hills of Anatolia, two along the coast of the Black Sea. Under these conditions it seemed unfair to record an impression of the country. Except in the few large towns, the population sensibly kept themselves indoors; the fields lay sodden and abandoned, while the coastal resorts were as bleak and uninviting as Brighton Front on a New Year's Day.

> Another landscape occurs through the mist.
> One tree marks the horizon.
> Lorries rumble past us
> Up the road to Trebizond
> And I travel silently, remembering

The last vivid evening in the city
Through the cold rain.
The road is almost empty—
Men sparse as trees, birds fewer,
But everywhere mist, a wall, against which
Memories burn like lamps.
The land plummets from the road
Into dim mysterious valleys—
In twenty kilometres nothing
But hills, a lake, a rusted shell;
Only the road reveals itself,
A black ribbon tying the past to cloud.

Even this cloud, however, had its silver lining: Fabian was forced to admit that in the light of their inadequate performance against the elements in Bulgaria, there was no question of sleeping in the tents. Little provision had been made in our limited budget against such a contingency: on Greg's calculations, 15p was was the most that we could afford for a bed. This involved us in some anxious haggling, conducted sometimes in a variety of languages. The best bargain was struck in a small village just short of the coast: what appeared from the outside as no more than a hole in the wall offered two rooms which, if a trifle cramped for the eleven of us, were both clean and warm—a fact which no doubt had something to do with the owner being an old soldier (as he was not slow to inform us, bringing round a boxful of campaign medals for our inspection). This was more than could be said of our choice in the steel town of Karabok, a draughty, stone-floored establishment which was shaken to its foundations every few minutes by lorries roaring past with enormous loads of rods and bars.

We suffered two setbacks in the hills; this was hardly surprising as we were now confined to what the map coyly described as 'limited weather roads'. The first occurred when we dropped down from Karabok towards a river which had already burst its banks and was spreading across the valley floor like a melting bar of milk chocolate. As we levelled out alongside it we suddenly ran up against a long line of lorries and buses stretching out of sight round the next corner. We got out to investigate and found the drivers and passengers staring disconsolately into a gap some thirty yards wide where the road had subsided and been carried away down the slope. Nobody seemed in the least interested in remedying the situation until a gang of peasants appeared on the far side, armed with shovels. A lengthy argument ensued as to the proper price of their labour.

Fabian, growing restive, untied our own spade from the roof and set to work with it. The reaction was instantaneous: he was made very forcibly aware that even in this unlikely spot the principle of the closed shop still applied.

'We're going to be here all day at this rate,' he concluded gloomily, 'and by the time that lot in front have got across they'll probably have to start filling it all in again.'

'I know,' said John, never lost for a suggestion, 'why don't we take the tarpaulin off the top and put it under the wheels as a sort of bridge? It ought to give them a pretty good grip.'

'I see: you reckon it's thirty yards long, do you?'

'No, of course I don't; we'd have to do it in stages.'

'And if I start sliding into the river in the middle of one of these stages, you'll come and pull me out, will you?'

'Well, I don't think that's very likely.'

'Well, I do.'

Bruce came up with a more modest proposal, born, perhaps, of native Yorkshire caution: 'I think you might make it if you keep right up to the top; it's only dropped a couple of feet there and looks reasonably firm to me.'

Fabian went to see for himself and returned more optimistic. 'You could be right; it's certainly worth a shot, anyway. The rest of you had better go on ahead and I'll pick you up.'

We crossed the gap and walked on another hundred yards before turning to watch the outcome. The Land-Rover appeared from the back of the queue and drove slowly to its head. The crowd converged on it to remonstrate, and in a gesture of appeasement Fabian reversed a few yards. Mollified, they resumed their negotiations. Suddenly he shot forward again and ploughed along what had been the upper verge of the road. For an agonising moment the Land-Rover teetered on the far edge as the trailer threatened to haul it back again into the abyss, then somehow regained its momentum and clambered out. Several of the shovel party gave chase, gathering up missiles as they ran. We just had time to scramble aboard before the first stone rattled against the back door.

The second mishap came a day later, on a stretch of road undergoing intermittent repair. We caught up with a white Fiat and moved out to overtake. It swerved off to the right as if to let us pass, then without the least warning pulled back again across our bows. J.C. swung the wheel over as hard as he could, but he never had a chance; the two vehicles locked together in a screeching crunch of metal, slewed across the road and finished up a couple of feet from a rock face.

When they were eventually parted the Land-Rover's wing wore a somewhat aggrieved expression, while the driver's door of the Fiat was completely stoved in. The driver himself was a man of considerable bulk, who had some difficulty in extricating himself from the steering wheel; however, he appeared unscathed by the accident, even amused, and with a wealth of gesture and a more limited command of English showed himself refreshingly free of the knock-for-knock, admit-no-wrong attitude inculcated by British insurance companies into their policy-holders.

'The rain is very bad, yes?'

'Yes,' agreed Fabian warily.

'It makes me like a blind man.'

'Evidently.'

'I see you not at all. I am so sorry.'

'That's all right. Could I have a look at your insurance?'

The other's genial features went blank. 'Insurance? Sorry, I am not knowing what you say.'

'You know, it pays for the damage.'

'But I am paying for the damages. How could I not? As my name is Mahmud, I am a man of honour, I swear to you by the sword of the Prophet—'

'Yes, yes, of course you are, but we happen to be going rather a long way and we might be in India before we can get it repaired.'

'In India?' He laughed infectiously. 'Ha, I see now what you think, but have no fear, my friend: the work will be done in my town, I swear to you.'

'Where's that?'

'You will find it very easily; it is a very big town, very important. Follow me and I will show it you.'

He eased himself back again behind the steering wheel and roared off. Fabian, fearing the worst, accelerated after him, and all but rammed him a second time as he made another, equally unheralded turn. He made several more, and at last the reason for his behaviour became clear: namely, that he was engaged in some supervisory capacity over the roadworks.

Fortunately, 'his town' proved to be only a few miles further on.

He led us through the puddles of a deserted market to a line of corrugated-iron shacks. A crowd of boys were picking about in the mud outside for such choice items of offal as worn-out windscreen wipers and defunct head-lamp bulbs. Mahmud entered and tugged at a leg projecting from beneath the chassis of a venerable Mercedes until the whole torso came into view. Its owner vented his resentment at such treatment on the boys who had now surrounded the Land-Rover, bringing a starting handle to bear on them with the same gusto that our guide at the Santa Sofia had shown with his umbrella.

'The work will take two hours,' Mahmud announced after a lengthy conference.

Fabian looked sceptical. 'I'll believe that when I see it.'

'It will be done, I swear to you by the sword—'

'All right, all right.'

He was as good as his word: when we returned at the appointed time, the whole wing had been dismantled, beaten out into its former shape and replaced. Only a few scratches in the paintwork remained to indicate that it had suffered anything amiss.

In the interlude Bruce and I set out to divert ourselves once more with bat and ball. At lunch the previous day we had put up the stumps in a spot which we appeared to have entirely to ourselves, but almost before the first ball was bowled a dozen cloth-capped spectators had materialised from nowhere and remained in rapt silence until the close of play. Now we were to make a still greater mark. Some of the boys followed us as we sought a pitch in the higher, puddle-free part of the town; others quickly added themselves to this strange procession until we had an audience of a size to make the average County Secretary drool at the mouth. Play eventually began in a square overlooked by a large building which turned out to be the local school, for within a few minutes every window was crowded with small heads. The authorities apparently came to the sensible conclusion that no more teaching was going to be done that morning: the windows suddenly emptied and their occupants poured into the square. All attempts to explain to them the concept of a 'boundary' were to no avail; it was as much as we could do to persuade them to withdraw far enough to allow the ball to reach the bat. Soon the inevitable happened: an uppish cover drive caught one of them full in the face. His howls of anguish evoked no sympathy from his fellows, only delighted laughter, indeed they gave the impression that this was really what they had come to see. The competition to retrieve the ball was intense, and it was often several minutes before the game could restart. One youth, older and more confident of his English than the rest, asked to be allowed to bat and after being instructed in the grip and the technique of the forward defensive shot developed quite an aptitude for the game. When the two hours were up, he pleaded with us for some memento of our visit. I went through my wallet and found that I still had my MCC membership card with me. It seemed the perfect answer: no one at home would object, surely? The season was over, after all.

However, the vengeance of the gods of the Long Room was as swift as it was terrible. At our next lunch-stop on a roadside embankment Bruce offered a sharp chance to where second slip would have been; the ball disappeared over the edge and was next seen bouncing towards what had been a small stream but was now a brown torrent. We raced to cut it off, but it just eluded us; we could only stand and watch as it was borne off to the Black Sea.

It was not until we reached Delhi that play was to be resumed.

Another dream died at Trebizond, which, admittedly on the briefest of inspections, appeared much like any of the other provincial towns through which we had passed, and looked out over dockyards instead of the expected beach and promenade.

We turned inland for the monastery of Meryemena, one of the last strongholds of Byzantine Christendom to hold out against Islam. We soon saw why: it lay at the head of a ten-mile gorge, accessible only by a rocky track which hugged one side precariously, in places hardly wider than the Land-Rover.

Our progress was made still more hazardous by a confrontation with a timber lorry; we were left in do doubt as to who was expected to reverse, at which point several of us opted to complete the journey on foot.

At last we drew up beside a wooden hut displaying a few postcards. The rain had finally relented, although the cloud still hung low and menacing. Just beneath it we could see the monastery peering out from the cliff face which rose almost vertically from where we stood.

A gnarled and wizened old man—J.C. dubbed him, not implausibly, the last of the monks—emerged to relieve us of some money and hand over in exchange an enormous ring from which hung an equally enormous key; it must have been a foot long, and its very weight was sufficient to explain why he chose not to accompany us. I asked him how long the ascent would take, and his finger indicated an hour on the dial of my watch. John doubted whether the pilgrimage to a rival god was worth the time and effort, but the majority (including even Malcolm) decided otherwise.

> At this moment by the wayside,
> Life condenses into effort and rest.
> The others go ahead and I sit
> Following the valley down with my eyes,
> A thousand feet to the river.
> On the opposing side, the green and amber
> Of pines and autumn birches,
> In the gulf cloud hangs like steam
> From subterranean geysers, and above
> The vacant eyes of the monastery
> Look down from its ruined face.
> As I wait, another passes me and I hear
> The jingling of his keys and chain
> Going away up the hill, to unlock
> A millenium of dust and silence
> For those who go before.

The cloud began to close in again as we zigzagged upwards through the dripping trees. Now and then we caught a tantalising glimpse of our goal through the branches and soon every corner seemed as if it must be the last, but the old man's estimate proved correct to within a minute.

A long flight of steps carved from the rock led up to a massive wooden door; it took the combined efforts of three of us to turn the key in its rusting lock. The outer buildings which had evidently served as the monks' living quarters had long ago lost their roofs and had been reduced to empty shells, but the inner sanctuaries had been gouged out of the cliff face and so protected from the elements. The brilliant frescoes that decorated their walls and ceilings had suffered at the hands of other enemies: firstly, of Islamic fanatics who had in most cases fortunately confined their attentions to the faces, and secondly, of those more recent desecrators who, following the pernicious example of Byron, had incised their names on any available surface. Those that had survived still radiated an extraordinary freshness and tranquillity; to consider the conditions under which their creators must have lived, perched in this outlandish eyrie, was to realise just how foreign the concept of Faith has become to the present age.

We climbed all next morning to a pass of six thousand feet, a height we were to maintain until we dropped down to the Caspian beyond Teheran.

During the ascent, Malcolm grew steadily less and less boisterous, finally lapsing into silence; even the burgeoning stubble could not disguise his pallor.

Suddenly he shouted to Fabian to stop.

'What's up, Malcolm?' Heather asked, seeing a chance to retaliate. 'Can't stand heights, is that it? I think he wants to go home, Fabian.'

'Stop!'

We were still on the move when he shot out of the back door clutching the communal roll of lavatory paper and made for the nearest bush (over a hundred yards away, thanks to the mountainous terrain) with a speed which belied our previous opinion of him.

As we waited for him to re-emerge, June too was similarly taken short and vanished rapidly from sight. This dual performance continued into the afternoon at half-hourly intervals. The rest of us began to wonder whose turn it would be next, and recalled uneasily the odds and ends which had gone into the previous evening's stew; some Yugoslavian sausages were agreed to be the obvious culprit.

However, the day claimed no further victims, and eventually Malcolm confessed that after coming down from Meryemena he had satisfied his thirst in a small stream behind the janitor's hut. June went into a huff when it was suggested that she might have done the same—of all people, she knew better than that. How then had she succumbed? Speculation on the matter gave rise to considerable ribaldry.

The joke was soon lost on me, however, for as dusk set in, so too did the familiar symptoms of flu.

'Is there any danger of us camping tonight, Fabian?' The question was a measure of my despair, for we had not passed a building of any sort for fifty miles.

'Why not? Wait till we get back here in February, when it's under four feet of snow; then you'll really find out what it's like to be cold.'

'I'm not sure that I'm going to,' I muttered miserably, and shivered out a sleepless night.

The terrain grew steadily more barren and desolate, but even if we had passed through the Hanging Gardens of Babylon that day, I don't think I'd have noticed. My sole concern was to contrive for myself a position in the Land-Rover which would allow me some sleep, but even with the help of aspirin this was no easy matter: it was not my turn for the front seat, the one recognised place of comfort; the middle row I had already found hopelessly cramped; the medicine chest, which was kept under the seat at the front of the rear compartment, made legs decidedly unwelcome in that quarter; I thus had to make what I could of one of the back corners. At first it seemed to hold some promise, and several times I managed to doze off. I was very soon to regret them, however: anyone not already acquainted with them should be warned of the two bolts which project from the rear door of a Land-Rover at a height precisely calculated to catch a nodding head an excruciating blow on the temples whenever the vehicle passes over the slightest bump, and on that road the bumps were more than slight.

We ended up on the lower slopes of Mount Ararat.

The snow on its volcanic cone glowed a delicious pink in the first light of dawn. A knot of children in charge of some goats already stood watching us intently. They edged gradually closer, attracted perhaps by the sight and smell of our breakfast; at any rate, they accepted our offerings of bread and marmalade and after some initial hesitation consumed them with evident relish. Not even John's polyglottery, however, could coax any speech from them; the most they would do was to point to a cluster of mud huts about half a mile away. Although this seemed unlikely to constitute an invitation, we decided that it was worth a visit, if only to find out how anyone was able to eke out a living from such unpromising surroundings.

One group of buildings was set a little apart from the rest, and its owner advanced towards us preceded by a menacing posse of large, hungry-looking dogs. The children withdrew towards the main village, leaving us to what seemed likely to prove a most unpleasant fate.

In a moment of inspiration, John produced his phrase book. Of the conversation that then passed between them even he claimed afterwards a hazy recollection, but whatever it was, it worked: the crisis passed, the dogs were beaten or kicked into truculent passivity and we were bidden to follow him on a tour of his property. He led us first to a patch of ground where a boy of no more than twelve struggled to control a primitive wooden plough drawn by two shambling cows; its share was so blunt, or the earth so hard, that on reaching the end of a furrow he was obliged to lift it clear while the cows turned before he could begin a new one. There was nothing to indicate what, if anything, had grown there before.

We were taken next to inspect his other livestock: sheep, goats, pigs, hens, all penned in a single walled enclosure. Four women attired in unexpectedly colourful dresses watched us shyly from the doorway; they appeared to be of widely different ages, and we could only hazard a guess as to their respective status.

The tour ended at a curious-looking kiln, built much in the style of a Kentish oasthouse. A stack of brown, rather unappetising cakes stood up against it; it was not clear what they were composed of, or whether they were the kiln's fuel rather than its products. To resolve the question, John picked one up and made as if to eat it. Our host's reaction was one of uproarious amusement, and he finally put us out of our doubt on the matter by grabbing a hen and squeezing it until it defecated.

The sight of the unfortunate bird's discomfort provoked him to still more convulsive laughter. Our experience of the Turk was now such that we would have been distinctly surprised if it hadn't.

4   A BORDERLINE CASE

The Persian frontier was less than an hour distant.

As we filled in our Turkish exit forms, a sign in the far corner of the compound caught my eye: Duty Free Shop. Closer investigation proved it to be no mirage (praise be to Noah?), but well-stocked with familiar brands of whisky. It lacked only someone behind the counter to serve me.

I approached the man in the Tourist Information Office. He was unshaven and clearly suffering the most monumental hangover.

'Excuse me, but I wonder if you can help me.'

I was answered with a hideous groan.

'Can you tell me when the Duty Free Shop opens?'

Two bloodshot eyes blinked at me sightlessly.

'The shop, drink, cigarettes,' I elaborated. 'When does it open?'

'No.' he said finally.

'What do you mean, no?'

'Is not open.'

'Yes, I can see that. When does it open, then?'

'One month.'

I mouthed some unprintable expression.

'Today begins Ramadan.'

'Ramadan?'

'The Fast. For one month, no drink, no smoke, nothing.'

For the first time I began to feel some sympathy for his condition.

'Are you sure?'

'Yes, I am sure,' he said, and groaned again.

The awful truth was confirmed for me by the Passport Inspector as he thumbed through my vaccination certificates against cholera and smallpox, unmoved by my distress. That's bureaucracy the world over, I reflected bitterly: as long as you had the right bits of paper on you, they were quite happy to sit back and watch you die on your feet.

An hour later we were cleared to advance the last twenty yards into Persian territory and here submit ourselves to the same lengthy examination.

During one of the several periods of inactivity I happened to look back over the barrier and noticed to my surprise a queue forming up at the counter of the Duty Free Shop (I had already satisfied myself that no such establishment existed on the Persian side). A moment later the man at its head came away with an armful of bottles and cigarettes.

I considered what my tactics should be. There seemed little change to be had from the surly-faced guards who manned the barrier, especially as my passport was now sitting on a desk somewhere awaiting its turn; the best hope seemed to lie inside the warren of offices which spanned the border. After several dead ends I came to a door and through its window recognised the Tourist Information Office; there was no sign of its previous occupant and it was empty except for an elderly sweeper who was making a tour of the ashtrays, picking out each stub and squeezing the remnants of tobacco into a leather pouch. I tried the handle, but it was locked. I then tapped on one of the panes to gain his attention, but he merely shook his head and moved on to the next ashtray.

Finding no other point of access indoors, I went outside and walked round the back to the customs shed. Packing cases stretched from end to end; there seemed to be no obvious point of demarcation. I walked down the row feigning a cursory interest and had almost got to the last of them when there was a sudden commotion and I turned to see three men running towards me, one of them a soldier brandishing a rifle. They were clearly in no mood to be trifled with, and I offered no resistance as I was frogmarched back to the other (Persian) end and roughly ejected.

I decided to have one more last shot at the Information Office. The old man had finished with the ashtrays and was now wiping down the tables. I tapped again on the widow and pressed a dollar note against the glass. It spoke a language he understood: he came over and after checking to see that he was unobserved, let me in. I took my place in the queue and was presently rewarded with a bottle of Haig.

My joy was short-lived: I returned to find the office locked and deserted, nor was there any sign of my accomplice. It was a nasty moment. Without my passport I was hardly going to get very far through the bureaucratic mill, which left only the barrier. I waited until a large, open-ended lorry was waved through, then followed as closely as possible in its wake.

It didn't work. The guards pounced on me and led me at the point of a bayonet before the Chief of Police. His features were not such as to reassure me: what little hair he still possessed was concentrated about his eyebrows, but their luxuriance could not conceal the hostile, gimlet-like quality of the eyes beneath them which now surveyed me. A brief, staccato conversation ensued between him and the guards, at the end of which I was thoroughly frisked and my wallet placed on the desk along with my bottle.

Gimlet-eyes picked it up and shook it. A hundred and fifty dollars and my remaining lira fell out. He counted them carefully and put them to one side before passing on to the other contents, probing among them with a pudgy finger. My membership card of a London night club seemed to cause him most interest; he examined both sides minutely, even though the back was completely blank.

'English,' he concluded.

'Yes.'

'Your name is Raymond Revuebar?'

'No, Michael Montgomery.'

'Let me see your passport.'

I explained its whereabouts in terms which I thought to be incapable of misinterpretation. I was wrong.

'You have lost it?'

'No.' I repeated the explanation with little more success.

'Why are you here without your passport?'

'I just wanted to buy some whisky, that's all.'

'Whisky?'

'Yes. It's in this bottle.'

He unscrewed the cap and sniffed at it with some distaste. 'Why do you want this?'

'Because I am very ill.'

'You are ill?'

'Yes. I've got flu.'

'Flu? What is that?'

'Influenza: it's a very serious illness.'

'I do not think that you are ill. I think that you lie to me.'

'No, honestly—'

'I will tell you why it is that you have come here: you try the smuggling.'

'For one bottle of whisky?'

'Not whisky; hashish.'

'Hashish? Yes, of course, Pusher's my second name,' I said, entering into the joke; I had not suspected that the man had a sense of humour.

He banged his fist on the desk, causing my possessions to jump in the air.

'Mister Montgomery, this is not a thing for laughing; in this country the smuggling of hashish is a very, very bad crime.'

'But it's absurd. I told you, I only wanted this bottle of whisky.'

'Why then have you all this money?'

'Because I am going a long way—to Nepal, if you must know.'

'But you have no passport.'

'Look, I've already explained—'

'Where is the hashish? It will be better for you if you tell me.'

'I have not got any hashish.'

'You put it on the lorry, yes?'

'No, of course—'

'I am sorry you do not tell me the truth. For this you will go to prison for many, many years. But you are lucky: if they had found you in Persia, they would have shot you. And now I will send you to Agri.' (It had been the last major town, about a hundred miles back.)

He said something to my escort and I was seized by both arms and led away to the door.

At that moment, in the best tradition of high tragedy, the *deus ex machina* made his appearance in the form of Fabian, accompanied by a Persian official and, more welcome still, my passport.

After half an hour of excited argument and gesticulation, and to Gimlet-Eyes' undisguised disappointment, I was a free man.

When the border was safely behind us, Fabian turned to me and said: 'As far as I can remember, there's no duty-free shop at the next border, but if there is, you might consider giving it a miss.'

I conceded the justice of the suggestion.

5 PERSIA: POETS QUICK AND DEAD

That night we had our first experience of an institution which from now on was going to be an increasingly prominent feature of our journey, the *chaie khana* or teahouse. It was not altogether an auspicious one.

Our schedule demanded that we should be in Teheran the following evening, and the delay at the border, coupled with the clocks going forward one-and-a-half hours, meant that it was already dark before we got through Tabriz, our goal for the day. The first attempt at a camp site turned out on brief inspection to be the municipal dump. We drove on a further twenty miles searching in vain for another site before settling for the *chaie khana*. It offered an excellent compromise: in return for the protection of his roof, the jovial, bearded proprietor seemed to expect no more than that we should drink a certain quantity of his tea—which, being sweet and strong, was no hardship even for an eccentric like myself who normally forgoes both milk and sugar, especially when laced with my hard-won whisky. I say 'seemed' advisedly: even with the aid of John's phrase-book we were quite unable to establish any sort of common language, but merely grinned and nodded at each other rather inanely. The only other member of the household was a soft-skinned, bright-eyed boy who scurried in and out with sticks for the ancient stove, a formidable piece of ironmongery which all-too-vividly recalled for me my brief experience of a Catterick barrack room. He might have been taken for the son of the house had it not been for the lascivious glances which his appearance provoked from our host, suggesting a rather different relationship. We were shown into their sleeping quarters and invited to pass the night there on several rickety *charpoys* (wooden-framed string beds); however, most of us elected to bed down on the concrete floor of the main room. I congratulated myself once more on my foresight in bringing the air-bed, but it was not on this occasion to give me much solace.

I had been asleep for no more than an hour when my dreams were shattered by a blood-curdling shriek from somewhere close beside me. It was John.

'What was all that about?'

'Didn't you see it?'

'No, what?'

'Some horrible furry thing. It was sitting on my face.'

'Are you sure it wasn't your nightcap?' (He invariably wore his Peruvian balaclava to bed.)

'Of course it wasn't. It smelt revolting.'

'Well, perhaps it was our friend coming to kiss you goodnight.'

'Look, if you're going to be facetious. . . .'

'Wait a minute, I think I can see something behind you.' Blinking into the darkness, I had begun to make out a pair of eyes reflected in the dim glow of the stove. 'Give me the torch.'

A large ginger cat stared back at its beam, affecting innocence.

With typical feline persistence it waited only until John had resettled before returning to its chosen place of rest. Peace was not finally restored until the animal was taken protesting to the window and ejected.

Nor was it to last for long. A few minutes later a thunderous drumming on the door shook the building and a dozen of the most villainous-looking men imaginable poured into the room. It was impossible to tell whether they were already known to the proprietor, for it would clearly have been more than his life was worth to have raised any objection; after relighting the kerosene lamp, he withdrew again to his quarters. They dumped their baggage in a corner and with much rasping and scraping of chairs established themselves in a circle round the stove to prepare a meal. A pot of tea was followed in due course by a pan of stew which gave off an overpowering stench of grease and onions. Throughout, all twelve jabbered at each other at the very tops of their voices; they could hardly have been unaware of our presence, but the thought that we might be trying to get some sleep appeared not to have occurred to them. After a further round of tea, one of them launched himself into some nomadic saga.

On and on he droned into the night. Finally I could take no more and raised myself on one elbow to remonstrate. There was a sudden rip of material, a rush of air, and I hit the floor with a bump. Feeling no less deflated myself, I fumbled for the torch and inspected the damage: the pillow was split from end to end and beyond all hope of immediate repair.

It came almost as a relief that it was my turn to rise at 4.30 and prepare the breakfast.

Few had slept any better, and tempers were short. An argument soon developed over the day's route; Fabian proposed driving straight to Teheran, but Bruce had other ideas.

'Bloody hell, Fabian, don't tell me we're going right through Persia without a look at a carpet centre.'

'Well, we've missed out on Tabriz so you haven't got much option,' was the retort.

'We can go to Rasht which is the next best thing.'

'You can, but I'm not going two hundred miles out of my way for the sake of a few tatty rugs.'

'It would mean exactly another forty-five miles—I've worked it out, so don't try and bullshit me.'

'All right, but it's still an extra two days drive on that road.'

'Why the hell?'

'Because it's nothing more than a dirt track over the mountains, that's why.'

'The map makes it just as good as your road.'

'Balls.'

'Look here, mate, I'm telling you I can read a map as well as you can.'

'And I'm telling you I know the road and you don't.'

They stood glaring at each other over the Bartholomew.

'Why don't we have a vote on it?' J.C. suggested hastily.

'Right,' Fabian said, seizing his chance, 'who wants to spend another three days bouncing around on dirt tracks and sleeping out in the mountains, and who wants to get to Teheran tonight and have a couple of days rest?'

'Now look here, Fabian—' Bruce protested, but his cause was already lost; the promise of a bed, clean sheets and running water swayed even the loyalty of a fellow-cricketer. He looked at me as he might at a Lancastrian who refused to walk when caught behind the wicket. 'You needn't expect any more seconds of spud when I'm on cooks again.'

It was a fitting penalty for such treachery.

John then proposed a diversion further south via Hamadan and the tomb of the poet Baba Tahir, claiming that he had worked it out with a boot-lace and that it wouldn't add more than an extra twenty miles; however, a more precise method of calculation produced a figure ten times larger. He was only partly consoled by the promise that the projected route of our return through the south of Persia would take in Shiraz, the home of both Hafez and Saadi.

We covered more than four hundred miles that day, through what was now merely desert.

> As we pass, a boy stands
> With his hand raised in greeting
> And behind him the mountains murmur softly.
> The plain stretches endlessly ahead,
> Mustard-coloured, ochre, blossoming to green
> Beside small pools or where trees cling
> To water-courses for precarious life.
> In summer, this must be a burnt place
> And winter almost as harsh to it.
> The tiny fields are terraced into curves
> To hold the precious moisture in
> And the solitary tree is almost sacred.
> Rarely come the citadels of the plains folk,
> Then hard brown walls say 'This is mine',
> And they will cling there till the earth
> Turns barren and the rock itself crumbles.
> Beyond the long stockade go mournful camels
> Under measureless amounts of hay
> And herdsmen with their goats and sheep
> Who have scarcely marked the passing
> Of a dozen empires. Time for a breath.
> Move on.

There were few towns to detain us, but those that did all bore eloquent testimony to the power of oil in the world economy, the 'black gold' that lay beneath the surrounding sand. Their approaches were laid out in spacious avenues lined with lawns and rose gardens, terminating in roundabouts containing elegant fountains and monuments to the present monarchy or its distant Achaemenian ancestry. The centres sprouted with new buildings, and the facades of marble were by no means confined to the banks and other houses of finance; indeed, the general standard of architecture was such as to put its all-glass-and-concrete, nothing-matters-except-the-profit British counterpart to shame.

Not the least of the surprises were the sumptuous creations of the many patisseries. In one of these I was sufficiently bemused by the serried pyramids of whipped cream (not to mention the combined effects of flu, whisky and fatigue) to leave my wallet behind on the counter. It was half an hour before I realised its absence. I went back for it without the smallest hope of ever seeing it again—to have it returned to me, all one hundred and fifty dollars still intact; nor would my benefactor accept anything more than a packet of cigarettes as a reward.

I began to consider the so-called wily orientals a much-maligned race.

We reached Teheran at dusk—or, to be more precise, its outskirts at the height of the rush hour. Unfortunately the official camp site lay on the opposite side of the city and Fabian knew of no way of getting to it other than straight through the middle.

The avenues now became something rather less than spacious. However, this did not inhibit the outgoing traffic from encroaching further and further across the road until those going in the other direction were obliged to mount the pavement in order to make any sort of progress. Every yard of space was ferociously contested by half a dozen vehicles of all shapes and sizes ranging from oil tankers to hand-drawn carts. At intersections (few of which were governed by traffic lights, and when they were it made little difference) the confusion grew worse still, for the cross traffic took advantage of the smallest gap in the main flow to stake its claim. Finally we arrived at a point of total stalemate: a bus stood at right angles across the street besieged on all sides like a defenceless caterpillar fallen prey to a voracious army of ants. A policeman presently materialised and launched himself into the fray, but his flailing arms were only two amongst a hundred others and in the end he vented his frustration on an elderly pedestrian who had stumbled against his motor-cycle and knocked it into the gutter.

As we sat immobile, I noticed a hotel sign beckoning from a side street. John had seen it too; no words were needed to tell us that we were thinking along similar lines.

Not so Fabian.

'Why the hell can't you wait for the camp site? It's one of the best there is.'

'Yes, but it's still a camp site.'

'What does that mean?'

'Just that I'd rather have a roof over my head for a change, that's all.'

'You had one last night, didn't you? I don't know what more you want.'

'Well, I wouldn't say no to a bath.'

'You'll be lucky, unless you want to pay ten quid at the Hilton.'

'I'll still settle for a bed.'

'So the air-bed's not good enough for you?'

'Not for the time being: I split it last night.'

'God, you poor thing. So what are you going to do now?'

'See if I can get it mended, I suppose.'

'You might find it a bit rough up on the Khumbu Glacier if you can't. Are you sure you wouldn't rather fly back to London?'

Just for a moment he was nearer the truth than he knew.

He was right too about the bath: five hotels later we were prepared to admit that the word was no part of the Persian vocabulary. However, the sixth boasted a shower and a very reasonable double room for something like one pound fifty between us.

I left John to complete his unpacking and went in search of an English paper. On my way I passed the office of the Iran-America Society. The following poster was displayed in its window:

The Iran-America Society presents
W.D. Snodgrass
reading selections of his own poetry
9.00 pm

I made a note to pass the good news on, but it was not until we were half way through dinner that I remembered.

'By the way, while I was getting my paper I happened to see something about a poetry reading tonight. Fellow called Snodgrass.'

John's fork stopped suddenly short of his mouth.

'W.D. Snodgrass?'

'Could be; the name didn't mean too much to me, I'm afraid.'

'You don't know his "Heart's Needle"?'

'No. Should I?'

'It only won the Pulitzer Prize.' For the second time our relationship hung in the balance. 'I suppose you didn't notice who was giving the reading, did you?'

'The man himself, as far as I could see.'

'Snodgrass himself?' The fork returned again to the plate. 'Are you sure?'

'That's what it said.'

'Where's it being held?'

'The Iran-America Society place. If you go back to the main square it's about a hundred yards up on the left.'

'And when?'

'Nine o'clock.'

'What's the time now?'

'About ten to.'

He spooned up a mouthful of rice and was gone.

'Snodgrass is walking through the universe,' I woke to hear John inform the shaving mirror.

'I beg your pardon?'

'Snodgrass is walking through the universe,' he repeated, this time for my benefit. 'It's a refrain he uses in a poem in which he describes what it's like to find oneself born into the world lumbered with a name like Snodgrass.'

'It sounds as if he has a sense of humour, anyway. And he really was American?'

'Yes.'

'How very odd.'

'I must dash, if you don't mind. He told me of a bookshop where I could get "Heart's Needle" and I'm afraid there'll be a run on it after last night. See you this evening.'

The city offered few distractions that I could discover; even the Archaeological Museum was a disappointment, being in the course of a major reconstruction, but after a hot shower, two square meals and ten hours uninterrupted sleep on a sprung mattress, who was I to complain?

John, however, found some inspiration there.

The past, Mede, Persian and Assyrian,
Stares blankly from the ordered ranks
Of pots, artefacts and tablets
Bearing messages of doubtful meaning,
A eulogy, a curse,
A statement of accounts.
Here stands the statue of a king,
Whose very name is dust—my card says
'500 BC. Luristan. Bronze. Masculine.'
Beneath him in the case, his horse,
Also 'Bronze' and, I think, 'Masculine.'
Here tiny, sexual figures—virile still—
Though their tribe and progeny have vanished;
A green serpent—fangs bared—strikes at them
From a broken portal and in the midst of this
Monstrously alive—a hungry clay lion
Sits roaring terribly for ever.

The upstairs gallery is blue with Islam,
Pale, ancient carpets, murals,
Misty figurines and curious brass,
Rows of cross-patterned Amol bowls,
A chandelier from Mehrat,
A flowered plate from Isfahan,
A stained-glass window from Shiraz.
Suddenly, the afternoon sun
Strikes browns and greens
From ancient tiles and vases, and the glaze
Thaws from the rich colours underneath.
Here there are no men, no serpents
And no lions, but everywhere, colour, pattern,
And the eternal script—the Prophet's word.
The face of his God is undisclosed,
But the meaning of his message is not in doubt.

In other respects too he could claim to have had a more profitable day: his haul included an aluminium teapot, several packets of Earl Grey, a comprehensive guidebook of Afghanistan and the collected works not only of Snodgrass but also of Hafez, Saadi, Ferdowsi, Omar Khayyam and Baba Tahir (no less).

'Snodgrass is walking through the universe,' he repeated once more.

Hand in hand, it seemed.

We crossed the range of Demavend (itself another thousand feet higher than Ararat) and descended to the Caspian, where we bathed. The shoreline was as sedulously exploited as any Italian beach reserve, and just as featureless; no one landed any caviar. However the rise in temperature made a welcome compensation, and together with my success in patching up the air-bed with the tyre-repair kit led me to think that perhaps after all camping could be actually enjoyed.

Two further uneventful days brought us to Mashad, the last but hardly the least of Persia's cities. 'Mashad—City of Spiritual Inspiration' we read in the Tourist Office handout. 'In this central city of the Eastern Province of Khorassan, you will see the divine-appearing Shrine of Imam Reza with its golden dome and minarets, fabulous interior.' And for once the reality fell not far short; indeed, the whole complex (there are actually two domes, the other a no less brilliant azure), faced throughout with sumptuous ceramic tiling, seemed to sum up this land of dramatic contrast.

Being a point of pilgrimage to the Shi-ite sect of Muslims, the inner courtyard was strictly barred to the unbeliever. Not all those who crowded its entrances were there for the highest motives, however, and our pockets were soon bulging with cards advertising the 'turquoise factories' located in the bazaars which honeycombed the outer precincts. Their prices were made to look as attractive as their wares, but the innocent traveller should take careful note of the wording: without exception, all our purchases were found on subsequent analysis to be of fabricated stone.

On John's insistence, we drove a few miles out of the city to pay our respects to the tomb of Ferdowsi. Another surprise awaited us: several acres of what had been until recently merely dust were now laid out in flower-beds, lawns, lakes, shrubs and pines around a tall cenotaph of white marble. Whether the poet himself—a man reputed to have turned down an enormous bribe to go and live in the court of a rascally prince of whom he disapproved, and to have died in near penury—would have appreciated all this is open to doubt, but perhaps we should be grateful that in the century of the

Common Man such lavish recognition should have fallen to a poet rather than a politician.

6 AFGHANISTAN: INTO THE WILDERNESS

A comparison of the respective border posts provided an accurate indication of the changes that were to come. On the Persian side we found a neat, solid building, freshly whitewashed and manned by a squad of soldiers equipped with American helmets and rifles. Their superior was clearly not a man to abandon his pleasures even in so desolate a spot, for we were curtly informed that there was no question of his seeing us until he had finished his evening meal. We used the interval to enjoy what was to be our last taste of cream cakes for a long time.

When we returned, he was in a more expansive mood and leered lecherously at the girls and their passport photographs.

'I like English ladies, I like very much. English ladies very good, very beautiful. I like to marry English lady. You married, yes? No? Why you not married, you with the yellow hair? You like to marry me, yes?'

No one, least of all himself, regarded this as a serious proposal.

Ten miles of no-man's-land divided us from Afghanistan; it was not difficult to understand why neither country should be interested in laying claim to such a tract.

In the gathering dusk our headlamps picked out a striped log slung across the road. A slouching, unshaven figure emerged from the sentry box beside it, dressed in a baggy, serge uniform of indescribable scruffiness. He waved us into a yard backed by a line of low, stone buildings. The word Passports could just be discerned on one of them; a sheet of hessian flapped in the doorway.

The interior was lit by a single kerosene lamp. A number of turbaned tribesmen stood along one wall; they wore such Kafkaesque expressions of patient resignation that it was impossible to gauge how long they had been there. Fabian strode past them and behind the screen where the passport officer sat writing at a rickety desk. He looked up briefly and without speaking pushed across a blank form to us; we looked in vain at the pinched features for the bonhomie of his Persian counterpart.

We had got about three-quarters of the required details down on the form when he announced: 'Eight o'clock. You leave now, please.'

'But we've only got a couple more to fill in,' Fabian protested.

'I am sorry, today is finished, kaput.' He cleared the few papers from the desk and locked them in a drawer. 'You must come back at ten o'clock tomorrow.'

'But we've got to leave at eight.'

'That is not possible, I will be here not before ten o'clock, and now I am going.'

'Look here—'

But he rose and vanished rapidly into the night. The tribesmen too melted away. In his frustration Fabian screwed up the form and flung it through the open window.

As the Land-Rover retreated a little way into no-man's-land for the night, I went across the road to investigate a slightly larger building which proclaimed itself to be a hotel. According to John's guidebook, there were only two categories of hotel outside Kabul, 'good' and 'fair'. The former offered basic services (although these did not include soap or lavatory paper), electricity for at least part of the night, comfortable beds but bedding that was sometimes questionable and pleasant surroundings which made up for some of the other omissions; the latter were without even the pleasant surroundings.

The proprietor, squat and genial with a gold-studded smile, had been watching us from a table set in the entrance. He now advanced on me with arms outstretched.

'I am your friend Ali. What is your name?'

I told him.

His arms spread even wider. 'By my father, you are a famous man of war.'

'No, no, that's not me. He's rather older, for a start.'

'But you are his son?'

'No, nor any other relation.' I was not going to repeat the mistake which I made on the occasion of a late-night party in Rome which had ended in my falling into the Fontana di Trevi, much to

5　Mount Ararat

6　The Red City of Bamiyan

7   The dance of the riflemen

8   Two temporary Sikhs at Amritsar (author on right)

the indignation of a correspondent of *Il Tempo*, who reported me as shouting 'You can't do this to me! I'm Field Marshal Montgomery's nephew.' As I soon found out to my cost, Monty's popularity with the Italian people left something to be desired after his remarks on the martial qualities of their soldiery. Goodness knows what he might have said about the Afghan fighting man if he had ever seen that one example in the sentry box.

The arms relaxed abruptly. 'You wish to stay the night in my hotel?'

'Perhaps.'

'Is very good hotel.'

'Good rather than Fair?'

The question was lost on him. 'Yes, yes, very good. Very cheap also. Come, I will show you.'

Five rooms led off a central passage, each containing three or four *charpoys*. There was also a 'Special Room', a single with a separate washing area comprising a shower, bucket, lavatory and a pool of stagnant water.

'For you, yes?'

'How much is it?'

'Seventy Afs (there were then one hundred and eight to the pound). The other rooms are sixty only for one person.'

I hesitated, then remembered the night at the *chaie khana*: five pence seemed a small price to pay for the security of solitude. I'll take the Special.'

'Is good for you, Mister Montgomery. And your friends, they come also?'

'No, they've decided to camp.'

He raised a horrified hand. 'They are crazy.'

'Well, a little perverse, perhaps.'

'Camping here is impossible.'

'It's illegal?'

'No, but it is very dangerous, there are very many bad people outside at night: robbers,' he lowered his voice to a sinister hiss, 'assassins. Here you will be safe, but they will be murdered, I am sure. You must tell them.'

I did so, but the tents were already up and Fabian was in no mood to put himself in the hands of another Afghan for some time yet.

'They will surely die,' Ali repeated gloomily, counting to himself all the unfilled *charpoys*.

'What have you got to eat?' I asked, more in an attempt to change the subject than in any expectations on that score.

'Many good foods: soup, pilau, fruits. I will bring them to you if you go to the room at the end.'

'How soon?'

'Soon.'

My only fellow guests were four Canadians engaged in earnest discussion of the Watergate imbroglio. Introductions were further postponed by the evening's first power failure.

It was a long, long meal—as afterwards was my shower, for the water supply proved no more reliable than the electricity, and when it did come through the sprinkler head kept falling off.

Later a wind got up and the night turned surprisingly cold. I was obliged to supplement the one blanket allotted to me with the carpet. This was presumably what the guidebook had in mind when it referred to 'questionable bedding'.

The others rejoined me in the morning apparently untouched by any assassin's knife, and Ali soon dropped his show of amazement when he realised that they had come for breakfast.

At ten o'clock Fabian reported again to the Passport Office. Ten minutes later he was seen to re-emerge going through the motions of tearing his hair out. Between expletives, he explained the problem: every entry form bore a number, which was then recorded against the name of its recipient, and as we had already received one the previous evening, the old so-and-so refused point blank to issue us with another. If we wanted to get any further, we would have to produce the original—which by now could have been blown half way back to Mashad.

'You will not find it,' Ali predicted cheerfully, rubbing his hands at the prospect of further business. We fanned out about the compound, searching into ever more unsavoury corners, but without success.

Fabian retired to plead again with the official. John, phrase book as usual in hand, wandered over to a couple of small boys engaged in a desultory game of football with a bundle of paper bound up with string, and struck up a tentative conversation. Suddenly it occurred to him that this 'ball' might be worth closer inspection. He picked it up and holding it out of reach of the indignant footballers, began to unravel it.

There in its core lay the precious form. It was ironed out against the end of the trailer, completed, presented and grudgingly accepted. We were by no means yet free from the official's attentions, however, for the same man supervised our passage through the buildings marked Customs, Medical and Insurance; only at Police did we escape into other hands.

Shortly after midday we were cleared to enter Afghanistan. There was, as Fabian had envisaged, no Duty Free Shop, and to celebrate the occasion I shared a bottle of Coke with the disappointed Ali.

A great plain of sand and scrub stretched before us, from which mountains rose as cleanly as rocks from a still sea. There were very few signs of life: an occasional nomadic encampment of black sacking or, even rarer, a conglutination of mud huts (what on earth did their inhabitants find to live on?); the odd party of travellers on foot (where were they going to or coming from?); and hundreds of camels (whom could they belong to?).

The temperature inside the Land-Rover rose to uncomfortable heights, and the ventilation system soon proved to be no match for eleven perspiring bodies. We had every reason to be grateful, therefore, to the Russians and Americans who, with whatever motives, had between them completed a modern, concrete road to Kabul, eight hundred miles away. (There is a more direct route across the Hazarajat range, but it is only open at certain times of year and then only to the hardiest adventurers. Fabian expressed an ambition to come back and do it on his motor bike.)

After two hours we arrived at what appeared to be another mud village, but which was announced by a sign (the first we had seen) to be Herat, the country's second city, already important enough in 330 BC to have led a revolt against Alexander, prized later by Ghengis Khan and Tamurlane and finally chosen as the seat of the Timurid Empire. The concrete gave way to a narrow dirt track.

Advancing cautiously through clouds of dust raised by herds of sheep and goat streaming past us, we emerged suddenly into a clearing dominated by six towering minarets, seemingly erected quite haphazardly. The guidebook explained the mystery: they were the last remains of a great complex of mosques built in the fifteenth century under the direction of Tamerlane's daughter-in-law and described by Byron as 'the most beautiful example of colour and architecture ever devised by Man to the Glory of his God and himself'. The mosques had been demolished by the British in 1885 when under fear of Russian attack (and with them his lordship's signature?), and it was no surprise to learn that three other minarets had subsequently collapsed, for the six survivors looked as if they might do so at any moment; very little remained of the blue tilework which used to cover them.

As soon as we disembarked, swarms of small boys converged on us demanding 'baksheesh'. Some offered in return to take us on a tour of the sights, but most of them were simply begging. One beckoned us towards a minaret, insisting that he could take us to the top. We watched him shin up thirty feet of crumbling brick to the first aperture, but no one was persuaded to follow. A nauseous, lavatorial stench wafted across from a cluster of black tents nearby and we moved on.

After a line of primitive shops the track turned into the main street. The first impression was one of a bustling thoroughfare, but this was soon seen to be an illusion: the bulk of the traffic was made up of pony traps, and most of these carried no passengers.

We stopped again to lay in supplies. John and I were cooks for the day, and we set out for the shops in a mood of some pessimism. One look at the shrivelled, fly-blown haunches hanging from the butcher's rail was enough to decide us on a strictly vegetarian menu. However, the grocers' stalls were surprisingly well-stocked in the sort of items that I recalled seeing on the shelves of the village store of my Devon childhood: Oxo cubes, Huntley and Palmer biscuits, Bovril, Cow and Gate condensed milk, Ovaltine, Camp Coffee, Cerebos Salt, Colman's Mustard, Worcester Sauce, Brasso, Kiwi boot polish—and even, to John's delight, tins of Liebig's corned beef.

'That's great; now I can do a sort of Boeuf Bourgignon,' he crowed.

'They look a bit rusty to me; God knows how long they might have been here.'

'That doesn't matter: they found some of Scott's stuff in the Antarctic last year and it was still in perfect condition.'

'Yes, but it would have been slightly better refrigerated there.'

'They'll be all right, as long as they're still sealed properly and we can soon check that. All I need now is some bay leaves. . . .'

He did not, of course, find them.

As we prepared to depart, a fanatical-looking beggar leapt up on the bonnet and launched himself at the windscreen with a wet rag. For all his energy, he only succeeded in working the dust up into a thick, obfuscating paste. Nothing, however, could convince him that his services were unappreciated until we drove off, flattening his kettle, which he had left under the front wheel. His misfortune was greeted with hysterical laughter from everyone else present, but he was soon to have his revenge.

We left Herat through an avenue of optimistically planted pines—very few had lived to reach maturity—and emerged into a raging sandstorm. Although we slowed to half speed and shut every window and air-vent, a pile of sand built up steadily on the floor at the back. Presently someone opened the door to release it. John shouted an agonised warning, but he was too late: out rolled his teapot and disappeared beneath the trailer.

He went back to retrieve it, and returned holding up a neatly-rolled strip of aluminium.

We reached Kandahar late the next afternoon.

The atmosphere of somnolent decline was even more marked than it had been at Herat. Apart from one or two venerable buses, the pony traps had the main street to themselves. At the central crossroads a policeman in a faded uniform stood on a canopied dais supervising the traffic; every so often he would give a blast on his whistle in a forlorn attempt to advertise his presence, but the effect was rather to emphasise the latter's absence. How the town had come to lend its name to a snob Alpine ski club was not immediately obvious to me.

In the intervening three hundred and fifty miles we had passed only one community of any size, a caravanserai called Dilaram which boasted a single petrol pump and a quite modern hotel which, however, appeared to be entirely deserted. There was an unexpected air of bustle and festivity about the place, and we soon saw why: the fair had come to town. It consisted only of a few simple roundabouts and Ferris wheels, all hand-made from wood and hand-operated, but the interest and excitement which it generated was intense: this was clearly as much in the way of organised recreation that people in this part of the world ever came by. Everyone was dressed in their very best, which often included colours of blinding brilliance—even the womenfolk, who until now (if seen at all) had been rigorously confined to their black robes and yashmaks. My camera was evidently something of a novelty, for whenever I raised it to take a photograph I was at once besieged by small boys who jumped up and down in front of me waving their arms. In the end I was reduced to the rather tiresome stratagem of walking off from my chosen point of vantage, then sprinting back to it in the hope of outrunning them. Brisk business, mostly in melons, was being done in the adjacent market, and a long line of lorries were drawn up on the roadside. They were all at least twenty years old (most of them were early prototypes of the Bedford three-tonner that I had lurched about Catterick in during my all-too-brief career as Regimental Ration Stores Driver), but they had been maintained with such loving care that they looked as if they might have left the factory yesterday. More remarkable still was the elaborate decoration which took up every inch of their chassis; 'art galleries on wheels' would not have been an over-fanciful description. Each bore a different motif: birds, flowers, animals, signs of the Zodiac, etc. Pride of place perhaps went to the one with a continuous frieze of lions and tigers whose eyes were represented by coloured electric bulbs set in the paintwork and wired to the lighting system; it would have jammed the Southend Arterial Road solid with envy.

Dilaram apart, our only other human contacts came at the military road-blocks dotted every fifty miles or so along the road, and comprising as often as not no more than a rusty chain and a decrepit, windowless shack. The standard of turnout of the poor wretches who manned them was, if anything, lower than that of the sentry at the border, but the thought of such a posting would surely have softened even the Field Marshal's tongue.

At similar intervals we passed pathetic-looking cemeteries laid out beside the road. The graves were marked by a simple pile of stones and a sliver of slate for a headstone; their proximity indicated a high rate of infant mortality.

Otherwise, we saw nothing.

Not even camels.

An unnatural silence had fallen on John. All day he had hidden himself behind his guidebook; not a single anecdote, or operatic aria, or quotation from the collected works of Snodgrass had passed his lips. We put it down to grief at the loss of his teapot.

We ought to have known better.

It was not until we were sipping our after-dinner Nescafé and expressing ironic sympathy with the couple whose turn it was to wash up—always the most pleasant moment of the day and calculated to find Fabian at his mellowest—that he rediscovered his voice.

'Fabian, I've been thinking—'

'No, really?'

'—we couldn't make a little diversion to Bamiyan, could we?'

'Is there another poet buried there?'

'Not that I know of.'

'Then why should anyone want to go there, then?'

'It just happens to be one of the very early centres of Mahuyana Buddhism.'

'We're not all Buddhists, you know.'

'No, I realise that, but there's still a lot there that might interest other people.'

'Such as?'

'There's the two colossal statues of the Buddha himself, for a start; the largest's a hundred and seventy-five feet high, which ought to be worth seeing. Then—'

'What exactly do you mean by a "little diversion"?'

'Well, I've worked it out—'

'With your boot-lace?'

For a moment it looked as if John's Irish blood would overboil, but fortunately it passed.

'—it'll only add on an extra day. According to this you turn off to the left about twenty miles short of Kabul and then turn right over the Hagijak pass. It's less than a hundred miles in fact.'

'Wait a minute, let's just have a look.'

Fabian got out the Bartholemew and spread it over the steering wheel. 'There's no road marked on here over that pass,' he announced, 'and the only one that I can see is at least three times as long.'

'It's made another mistake, then. You said yourself it was all to cock in Persia.'

'We'd look pretty stupid if we got there and found it wasn't.'

'I don't know, we'd soon find out. And at the rate we're going now, we're going to have three days in Kabul, and even Kabul can't be that interesting.'

Perhaps it was the justice of this last observation that struck Fabian; or perhaps it occurred to him that it would provide useful reconnaissance for his expedition by motor-bike; or perhaps his conscience was suddenly overwhelmed by the memory of John's feat of deliverance at the border; at any rate, he yielded.

'All right, let's have a vote on it, then.'

The ayes had it.

The turning would not, of course, be signposted. The guidebook put it at eighty-five miles beyond Ghazni, the last town before Kabul, but this knowledge was not as helpful as it might seem, for the milometer had long since packed up and the speedometer now chose this moment to go literally off its head: after several hundred frenzied circuits of the dial, the needle finally flew off.

After something like two hours (nobody was quite sure exactly when we had left Ghazni) a dust road could be seen leading off towards a gap in the mountains on our left.

A square, single-roomed building stood at the junction. Inside, a lone soldier was slumped across the table, asleep.

When roused, he jerked up and sat staring at us in silent terror. It seemed unlikely that anyone could possibly mistake us for the Afghan High Command on a lightning inspection, a marauding band of the dreaded assassins or even an advance party of another Mongol horde descended from the steppes, but it was several minutes before he had relaxed sufficiently to return Fabian's handshake.

'Kabul?' Fabian enquired, pointing north.

'Kabul, Kabul.'

'Bamiyan?' Pointing west.

'Kabul, Kabul.'

Fabian tried again, but with no more success; the word Bamiyan brought only a look of total incomprehension.

The Bartholomew was produced and laid out on the table in front of him, but it was soon evident that maps had played no part in his military experience.

On the grounds that there was no other turning to the left marked between Ghazni and Kabul, it was decided to risk it.

The soldier watched from the doorway as we set off, scratching his head in puzzlement.

As we entered the foothills, the scenery changed at last from one of utter desolation. The river Kabul led us through a succession of fertile valleys upwards to its source; poplars lined the road, and the fields on either side were assiduously cultivated. It was hardly surprising that such a relative oasis should bear signs of having suffered the regular attentions of those from less well-endowed territories; every hill was topped by a fortification of some kind.

We stopped in the first village to ask again 'Bamiyan?'

Even the smallest child nodded reassurance.

The greenery fell away again as the road rose into a series of ever tighter hairpin bends until the Land-Rover needed two or three attempts at them. Only now did John reveal the height of the Hagijak Pass: something over twelve thousand feet. Further questioning elicited the additional information that snow could block it any time from the beginning of November onwards. The winter's first falls did indeed extend low enough on the north-facing slopes to touch the road at several points, but the pass itself was clear—which was just as well. Even so we all had to get out before the Land-Rover could make it.

We plunged down its other side through ice-fringed streams and into the maw of a beetling gorge.

As we rounded a corner out of it, a great wall of red sandstone suddenly filled the panorama before us. It is difficult to find words which can adequately describe the full impact of the transformation—it was almost as if a pink filter had been dropped over our eyes. The whole face had been carved in relief by a natural process of erosion to form a series of fantastical pinnacles and buttresses. As we studied it more closely we could also make out man-made breastworks and crenellations running along the top of the ridge and leading to the main fortress built at its end to overlook the junction with the Valley of Bamiyan. This was Shahr-I-Zohak, so John informed us, 'The City of Zohak'—or, as Westerners would have it, the Red City, which had been raised in the Twelfth Century on the site of much earlier defence works by the Islamic Shansabani kings. In 1221 the garrison had blocked the advance of a Mongol army led by Genghis Khan's favourite grandson, who was killed in the ensuing battle. His grandfather vowed to avenge him by putting the whole valley to the sword, which he did the same year with typical thoroughness. The path up to it was lined with curiously shaped towers which had no apparent means of access except, presumably, by ladder. We passed through a tunnel hewn out of the rock and found ourselves in a vast complex of armouries, barracks, kitchens and warehouses, all still very much as they had been left over seven hundred and fifty years ago. The view from the ramparts of the three different-coloured valleys—one pink, one grey, one ochre—converging immediately below provided chromatic testimony to the site's strategic importance. The Zohak of its title had been a prince who as a result of being kissed by the Devil suffered the rather trying impediment of a couple of serpents sprouting from his shoulders—serpents, moreover, who insisted on a diet of human brain. When he was eventually incarcerated by some local-boy-made-good, they, deprived of their usual fare, turned on poor Zohak's head and fed on it until he died. Genghis Khan would surely have enjoyed the story.

The fields and poplars returned to mark the approach to Bamiyan itself.

As we entered the town, a sheer, almost smooth cliff rose to our right, its face pock-marked by hundreds of monastic caves, some of them still the home of nomadic settlements. The two Buddhas were set at either end; the smaller was undergoing extensive restoration and could not be seen for scaffolding, but the larger stood massive and unencumbered in its shallow niche. The head had been defaced down to a point just above the mouth; whether natural decay or Islamic fanaticism were to blame was unstated, although the guidebook did record a story of one Islamic conqueror ordering the legs to be knocked about. One had been sliced off up to the knee, the other almost as far as the hip; the forearms too were missing. Delicately moulded drapery covered the main torso; it still bore a few faint traces of the red paint that used to cover it.

The official, white-robed guide led us up a zigzagging path at the side of the cliff. A hundred and fifty feet up it disappeared into a small hole in the rock face and we groped blindly along a succession of stairs and galleries before emerging on the head of the colossus itself. The ceiling of the niche bore several colourful murals of Buddha surrounded by bare-bosomed dancing girls and musicians, most of them still in surprisingly good condition; perhaps they owed their survival to the mere fact of being out of

the reach of iconoclastic hands. Below us there was a forty-foot
drop to the shoulders.

The dating of the Buddhas is still the subject of heated
controversy, although they are generally ascribed to the Third or
Fourth Century, a period which saw the climax of Bamiyan's
importance as a caravanserai on the Silk Train between India and
the West. Its past glory found few reflections in the present town,
which was little more than a street of primitive, sack-veranda'd
shops lined with open drains.

We stopped briefly at the *chaie khana*, where John negotiated the
purchase of a china teapot, an act of awesome bravado; his hope
that no one would mind if he kept it in the medicine chest was not
fully shared by Heather, whose charge it was. A large dog of
uncertain pedigree and temper sniffed at our heels as we drank. In
a sudden show of affection the proprietor patted it on the head,
whereupon a considerable pall of dust (or worse) was seen to rise
from it. It was not a place to linger.

We returned eastwards via the Shibar Pass, a longer but less
arduous route, and passed the night in the unaccustomed seclusion
of a poplar grove.

Our rate of progress the next morning was governed by an
elderly bus carrying a full complement of passengers both within
and without; even had there been room to overtake, we would
never have been able to see far enough through the screen of dust
to do so. Eventually the bus in turn was obliged to fall in behind a
procession of riflemen, perhaps fifty strong, marching in no very
obvious order or uniform along the full width of the road and
accompanied by a piper and drummer who between them gave off
a sound not unlike that of a Scottish bagpipe band. At a given
signal the rifles—ancient, fearsome weapons, relics perhaps of the
North West Frontier campaign—were piled together on the
ground and the whole company linked hands to dance round them
in counter-revolving circles. Just when it seemed that vertigo must
get the better of them, they picked up their rifles again and
resumed the procession. After a further hundred yards the main
body halted and the front rank of three began another circular
dance, this time retaining their weapons and holding them upright
as firmly as any ballroom champion might his partner in the palais
glide. After two or three more circuits they suddenly hurled them

aloft, caught them, pointed them at the ground, leaped into the air themselves and fired. The result would have read just as well in a Civil Defence manual on atomic warfare: a blinding, searing flash, a billowing cloud of dense smoke and a devastating blast which bounced back and forth between the steep sides of the narrow valley. When the smoke finally cleared the three could be seen recharging their breeches with gunpowder before taking their places at the rear to await a second turn.

The effect on the senses was overwhelming for all of us except John, who appeared out of the smoke at the head of the procession, although even he declined the offer of a rifle. I tried several times to photograph the moment of explosion but it made me jump so much that I doubted if any of them would come out.

Perhaps I shouldn't have bothered anyway; somehow, this was exactly how I had always imagined that the average Afghan spent his day.

After this, Kabul was bound to suffer by comparison, and it did.

The river which bore its name did not serve as much of an advertisement: at this time of year it was little more than a stream and a pretty insalubrious one at that, although, incredibly, a number of brave souls were to be seen trying to wash themselves in it. The population of half a million made for a rather more thriving community than either Herat or Kandahar (both less than a quarter the size), but the transition between the old and the new was still at a somewhat uneasy stage; if cars were no longer a novelty, traffic regulations certainly were. In the centre the embryo of a modern capital was slowly taking shape; in the many gaps still to be filled sheep, goats and pigs browsed undisturbed on the inevitable refuse. Little could be seen of the royal palace behind its double lines of fortification, and there were few other buildings of distinction; most of the mosques were of recent and predominantly functional construction. The mausoleum and former palace of Amir Abdur Rahman, creator of the present state of Afghanistan, was perhaps the one exception: its crenellations and green cupolas gave it a quaint resemblance to the Royal Pavilion at Brighton.

I had dreamt of something rather different.

Like Teheran, however, if offered compensations of a more materialistic nature—which, after twelve continuous days on the move covering nearly two thousand miles, were not to be sneezed at. The Caravan Hotel was a modest establishment, and it was just as well that the man and wife who ran it with the help of their several children were expecting us, for we took up every bed that there was; on the other hand, their solicitude for our welfare was possibly such as to suggest that any guest was something of a rare event. They fell on the hideous pile of our dirty clothes and bore it off to the backyard to launder; they kept the wood-fired boiler roaring all afternoon until each of us had taken a lengthy turn under the single shower; and as if the mere fact of a mattress was not sufficient to guarantee our night's sleep, they sent us to bed on a vast meal of rice and mince.

After an equally imposing breakfast, we set out for the bazaars. At every corner men and even quite young boys sidled forward to accost us. 'You have dollars, mister? Pounds? You want rupees?' It was a question that was to follow us now all the way to Kathmandu, thanks to India's draconian exchange regulations which have created a flourishing black market in that currency. 'I give you very good rate: twenty-two rupees for one pound. Please, mister, come with me.' (Eighteen was the official rate.)

Fabian waved them all aside and led us into a narrow courtyard lined with poky little cubicles. At one end a large, plate-glass door spoke of something more important: this was the office of 'The Baron'. Behind a desk banked with telephones and calculating machines sat a sleek, corpulent man of perhaps no more than thirty-five, sporting side-burns of the trendiest length and exuding opulence and financial savoir faire with every move of his manicured fingers; he would have looked just as at home in one of those City foreign-exchange rooms with which the BBC love to illustrate each new sterling crisis. He spoke several languages with equal suavity: 'Hello, Mister Shannon, Sir. How are you today? Yes, I am well too. You wish one hundred thousand rupees? I will have them tomorrow for you, Sir, God willing. You are most welcome, Sir. *Pronto, Signor Rossi? Come stai, mi' amico? Si, si, sono benissimo, grazie. Quanto . . . ?'*

The sum total of our requirement, nearly five hundred pounds, was sufficient to distract him temporarily from his telephones. His fingers ran rapidly over the keys of a calculator.

'I'll give you twenty-three seventy.'

'You gave twenty-four last time.'

'Last is not this time. Take it or leave it.'

At Fabian's suggestion Greg made a tour of the other offices, but none of them offered more than twenty-three and the deal was concluded. Most of the bank notes were in a rather sorry condition, and we were to spend many hours sellotaping them together again—with unforseen consequences.

I left the bazaars unpossessed of either a carpet or an embroidered sheepskin and flicked through the brochure for other possible points of interest. Something caught my eye at the bottom of a page: 'The Kabul Golf and Country Club is nearby.' Was it really possible?

The Tourist Information office knew nothing about it. The British Embassy seemed the next best bet.

A fresh-faced Junior Secretary answered me: 'Yes, of course it exists: we opened it ourselves five years ago. I believe the Americans chipped in something towards it as well.'

'How do I get to it?'

'It's out towards the Kargha Dam. There's no bus, you'll have to take a taxi.'

'What's that going to cost?'

'Oh, a couple of quid, I should think.' He paused to consider me a little more closely. 'Actually, I'm going up for a round myself in a few minutes; I might as well give you a lift, I suppose.'

'Thanks very much.'

In the car he grew still more expansive: 'My usual partner's away at the moment, so you might as well play with me, I suppose. What's your handicap?'

'Ten.'

'I'll be giving you a couple of strokes, then. You'll probably need them: it's quite a sporting little course if you don't know it. This is it now.'

It was not immediately recognisable as golfing country; in fact, there was not a blade of grass to be seen, least of all on the 'greens' which were represented by black circles of oiled sand. I hired a bag of clubs containing four irons, two woods and a putter, and engaged a youthful caddy called Mohamed and dressed in a tweed jacket and orange Pathan trousers (they were rather like plus-fours and and as such, suited him quite well).

At the first hole my opponent (I never did discover his name) topped his approach; the ball rolled and bounced over fifty yards of stony ground and came to rest two feet from the pin.

'A good negress,' I remarked.

'Negress? Sorry, I'm not with you.'

'You know, a sleeping-with-a-negress shot: very satisfactory, but not what you boast about in public.'

'I'm not sure that's in awfully good taste.'

We played on in silence. Mohamed was a man of few words, confining himself to his fingers whenever he wanted to indicate what club I should take. On the second nine, however, he found his voice, repeating at ever decreasing intervals: 'Two hundred for carrying, one hundred baksheesh, one Coca Cola. Okay, mister?'

Arriving at the last hole all square, I hooked my drive slightly and the ball came to rest at the bottom of a deep trench. I hacked at its three or four times without making contact and conceded the match.

'Bad luck, but I can't think why you didn't drop out,' my opponent said, 'it says on your card you're allowed a free drop from a *jui*.'

'Yes, but I wasn't to know it was a *jui*, was I?'

'Well, you only had to ask and I'd have told you. By the way, forty's the standard rate for your caddy; don't give him any more or he'll begin to get ideas.'

I gave him fifty and he ran off beaming delightedly.

'Are you going to be here tomorrow? It's the monthly medal.'

'No, I'm afraid we're leaving after breakfast.'

'Pity.'

Only a Junior Secretary in the British Foreign Office could have meant it less.

It was Bruce's birthday, and John and I decided that it called for something more than rice and mince.

We found it eventually in a restaurant run by a man of German extraction: in addition to *Wienerschnitzel*, he offered some very palatable wine made locally by some enterprising Italians. We drank rather a lot of it, and were treated in return to a generous round of schnapps as we waited for the doorman to procure a taxi.

After what seemed a somewhat uncertain journey through the ill-lit streets, we pulled up in a large square.

'Caravan Hotel?'

Without warning, the driver burst into roars of maniacal

laughter. Tears streamed down his cheeks while we settled the fare and long after he had disappeared again into the night, his shrieks could still be heard above the drone of his engine.

We looked about us, and dimly something stirred in me to explain his mirth.

We were standing outside the gates of the British Embassy.

> The men are silent,
> A generation of hawks;
> The gun speaks for them,
> Sharp steel
> Opens a way for them,
> And as for the woman
> Blue-veiled and mysterious
> She brings food and love
> Obediently for her husband.
> I watched them sow maize
> In the fields beside the purple hills
> Where the ruined castles stand
> Whose arabesques shelter the birds
> And I knew nothing had changed.
> A group of wide-turbaned men
> Watched impassively as we went by
> And behind them the sky burnt a fierce blue.
> We passed into wooded country
> And in the silence as the light failed
> Someone said 'Look, the birches
> Have turned into mist'.

7 THROUGH THE KHYBER

After the Kabul Gorge, a dizzy plunge of over two-thousand feet between vertical walls of rock, the much-vaunted Khyber seemed an insignificance, made more irrelevant still by a railway running up to it on the Pakistani side.

Our descent to the plain of the Indus was greeted by parakeets, hoopoes (for brilliant and ridiculous pomposity, Aristophanes could hardly have done better in his choice of King of the Birds) and other, less welcome, winged species.

> I crush it with my hands
> And its blood stains me,
> Rich, red and familiar.
> It is the hundredth being
> I have crushed today
> *Remorselessly.*
> But wait—there is a whining
> In my ears—silence
> A tickle on my neck.
> Stab—*Crash—Blood*
> It is true I take a pleasure
> In this slaughter, but the blood
> Is familiar, as I said,
> And worse, it is mine—
> *Die, gnat, die!*
> I am tired of all this killing;
> I wish to doff my armour now
> And sleep. Pass me
> The insect repellent.
> Thank you.

The last Indo-Pakistan war was still recent enough to allow the border between the two countries to open only once a week, which gave us two days in which to do the intervening four hundred miles.

This was not to prove quite as easy as it might sound, even when granted an adequate road surface for most of the way. In every town and village we ran up against a dam of bulging lorries, overflowing buses, emaciated ponies meandering all over the road impervious to the tugs and blows of their drivers, whole families of small children staggering between the poles of top-heavy barrows, and through what gaps there were oozed trickles of wobbling, jingling bicycles. Whenever we stopped, we were instantly engulfed by a seething press of inquisitive humanity, and to walk even a few yards to a sugar cane stall became a major campaign; the girls complained loudly, too loudly perhaps, of pinched breasts and bottoms. Very occasionally a baton-swinging policeman attempted to come to our aid, but he might just as well have tried to cut the heads off a Hydra.

We reached Lahore, twenty miles short of the border, late on the second day. Approached from the north, it has to be said that the capital of the Punjab did not present itself in a very attractive light: a long line of noisome tanneries and glue factories degenerated into total dilapidation and squalor at the entrance of the old city walls. From its other side one would gain a totally different impression: gleaming new offices and hotels, broad avenues, flowered parks and those shrines of Empire, the race-course and cricket-ground; it was almost as if a line of apartheid had once been drawn across the middle.

After several fruitless enquiries elsewhere, we ended up at the Swat Hotel, an establishment which had clearly seen better days. It offered a bed at two rupees and a 'special bed' at three; a blanket represented the difference. John and I saw little prospect of sleep in either and decided to make further investigations of our own. The Intercontinental seemed possibly a little excessive at one hundred and fifty a head, and we were happy to settle for the clean sheets, modern furniture and torrential hot shower of the Uganda at eleven each.

There was an air of resentment at the Swat when we returned to report our find. 'The trouble with you two is that you've got too much money', someone was heard to mutter.

'I wish we had,' I retorted. We had only brought what anybody with any sense would bring to last four-and-a-half months, and this particular extravagance was costing us the equivalent of something like six shillings or two bottles of Coke—and if they valued the chance of a decent wash and a good night's sleep once a week at less than that, we didn't.

This observation silenced the criticism—for the moment, anyway. Greg and Bruce confided that only a sense of group loyalty prevented them from joining us, an argument which failed to stir our consciences.

When we met up again in the morning, we found the others somewhat subdued. Bruce presently explained that he had pulled his bed out a little from the wall and had found beneath it a pile of something very, very unpleasant.

Although a dawn start saw us at the border only a little after eight, a considerable crowd had already preceded us both by car and foot, and stood in a queue three deep at the Immigration Office. Fabian was variously reported as being 'near the front', 'at the front' and 'through', but nine, ten and eleven o'clock all came and went without result, except that a pair of vultures took up station in a palm tree overhead. It looked as if they were on to a good thing.

At last, just before noon, a customs official arrived to inspect the Land-Rover.

'How many peoples are there travelling in this car?'

'Eleven.'

'Eleven?' he repeated, incredulous.

It was a rich moment.

We advanced all of one hundred yards to join the line of vehicles queuing at the Indian border.

As we inched forward, a long file of porters went past with sacks of rice on their heads which they were transferring from a Pakistani lorry to its Indian counterpart on the other side; their expressions of total apathy suggested that they had been engaged in this ever since the 1947 partition of the two countries.

An hour later we reached the checkpoint. After considering our passports at some length, the guard poked his head through Fabian's window to count us.

'I see only ten peoples here; who is the one people missing, please?'

It was a superfluous question, as John's lack of a watch had already proved on numberless occasions. Nobody had noticed him slip away; where could he have got to this time? Was he in India, Pakistan or somewhere in between?

The car behind began to hoot.

For the first time Fabian declared himself at a loss. If we gave up our place in the queue we would almost certainly not get through that day and so would be stuck in Pakistan for another week; on the other hand if we went on without John (assuming that we were allowed to) it was doubtful whether they would then let him through on his own. We would then have to go through Indian customs, re-cross the border, go through Pakistani customs, be cleared again for departure. . . .

'By which time there'll probably be another war on,' Bruce remarked with a certain journalistic relish.

The porters approached again with a fresh load, but this time there was an intruder in the line.

It was John, carrying not rice but beads. He looked exceedingly pleased with himself.

'I've just had a great bit of luck,' he announced, 'I got talking to this busload of Danes going the other way and one of them happened to mention he was trying to flog off some Tibetan stuff he'd picked up in Kashmir, including this—quite a bargain for fifty rupees, don't you think?'

'No, John, I do not,' Fabian told him with chilling emphasis, 'and I want to have a little talk with you.'

He led him out of sight behind the trailer. Their ensuing conversation was, I imagined, not unlike that which once took place after the master in charge of a school party to Athens had spotted me making an illicit entry into the Acropolis via the branches of an olive tree growing horizontally out of the sheer rock-face (he threatened to send me home by the next boat). At any rate, we heard no more about the beads that day.

And so we arrived in India.

After a picnic lunch in the company of several hundreds, we stretched out in the sun to while away another four hours.

Suddenly we were shaken from our slumbers by the thunderous bellowing of a familiar expletive, followed a few seconds later by another, even louder.

'*Fuck!*'

All eyes turned on a bearded, Teutonic figure brandishing a piece of paper in the faces of a knot of customs men.

'I have been here five hours,' he raged, 'and still you do not have my children on the form.'

He then threw it to the ground and jumped on it. This action brought a senior official running to the scene in an equal state of excitement.

'Please, what do you think you are doing? That form is the property of my government, and if you insult it like that you are insulting my government also. In India we do not like people who are insulting our government.'

'I have been here five hours: *five hours.* Do you understand that?'

'I don't care; you cannot behave like that. Maybe in your country you can behave like that, but in this country it is very bad.'

'Look, I just want to export my children; I don't want to leave them to rot in your lousy country.'

'You be careful: if you keeping talking like that you can go away and come back again next week, and if you are still saying such things I will send you away again, and so on and so forth. It is nothing to me how long you are staying in my country; maybe if you spend all your life here you will learn to behave well.'

The German gathered himself for a reply, then appeared to think better of it and retired to simmer in his Volkswagen.

The incident seemed to have some effect on the other side too, for the pace of the queue now quickened perceptibly and in another hour we were once more under way.

If anyone had any doubts that Islam and the abstinence of Ramadan were now behind us, they were dispelled by the time we got to Amritsar. In the space of those thirty miles we passed three lorries which had met with recent and spectacular disaster, overtook another carrying a crane whose arm was scything through electric cables with brilliant effect quite unnoticed by the driver, and followed for over a mile two crowded buses being driven flat out alongside each other, urged on enthusiastically by their respective passengers; when they arrived at a blind bend still locked together, even Fabian's flinty nerve wilted and we pulled up on the verge. Neither of them was seen again, although the next day we did read in the paper of a fatal bus crash in which eight people had been burnt to death, 'presumably women and children.

Police are now looking for the driver, who ran off across the fields before they arrived at the scene of the calamity.'

We stopped for the night on the far bank of the River Sutlej, a tributary of the Indus. For the first time we felt warm enough to dispense with the chore of putting up the tents.

As we sat eking out a meal of potato omelette (it was no fault of the cooks: the previous day in Pakistan had been declared 'meatless' by government decree, and we were not to know that we would have time to shop in India after crossing the border), a scooter bounced towards us over the dry scrub and slewed to a whining halt. Its rider, a majestic figure in a dazzling green turban, dismounted and strode across with ominous resolution.

'What are you doing on my land?'

Fabian affected innocence, albeit inconvincing. 'It's your land, is it?'

'Of course it's my land: it was the land of my father, and of grandfather also before him.'

'I'm sorry, I didn't know.'

'You had only to ask: everyone here knows that this is my land. You must go immediately, please.'

'What, now?'

'Yes: I cannot have strangers on my land without my permission.'

'We're prepared to pay.'

'Pay?' He dissolved into convulsive laughter. 'You must think us Indians a very funny people to make their guests pay for our hospitality.'

'But—'

'You are my guests, of course, and I am happy for you to stay here as long as you wish. I must beg your pardon: I have been drinking with friends and I was playing a little joke. Allow me to present myself: I am Captain Bhullar, formerly of the Fifth Indian Cavalry Regiment. I was at Sandhurst College for one year, you know; I like England very much, especially your pubs. And now all of you must come and have a noggin with me in my local.'

'I'm afraid some of us will have to stay and do the washing up.'

'But you have women to do that.'

'It's not actually their turn tonight.'

'You telling me that men are going to do the work of women?'

'Yes.'

'I cannot believe it. Why have you brought them if it is not to do such things?'

Nothing we could say was going to answer the question for him. The girls took it that the invitation did not extend to them, and it was a much depleted party that set out with him on foot to the village.

The 'local' turned out to be no more than a collection of rough wooden benches and tables set under an awning of sackcloth. We were served with raki, a rather insipid but nevertheless potent rice wine; water was also provided, but in the absence of Heather's Sterotabs the consequences of taking the raki neat seemed the lesser evil.

For over an hour our host regaled us with shell-by-shell accounts of tank battles (he had fought in both the '65 and '70 border campaigns).

'Do you get many snakes round here?' Bruce interposed quickly when the last Pakistani Patton Mark Five had been knocked out.

'Snakes? I should say so, my dear fellow: the whole place is just crawling with them.'

'Cobras?'

'Naturally I am speaking only of cobras: all the others we treat just like little fleas.'

'And do you get many deaths from them?'

'Yes, many, many. Every year at least two people from the village die. My own grandfather was bitten.'

'And he died as well?'

'Of course: once you are bitten, there is nothing that you can do.' He gave Bruce a hearty slap on the back. 'Don't be so worried, my good fellow: they have all gone to sleep now in the ground for the winter. But by the river you must still be careful: once I was just getting into the water for a bathe when I saw this bloody great snake rolling straight for me. I don't mind telling you, I buggered off, just like any Paki out of his turret. There was this battle. . . .'

We all looked at our watches simultaneously.

'Perhaps we ought to be getting back now.'

'Balls. You are not in England now, my friends; I am not going to say to you "Time now please, gentlemen". Here we can drink all night if we wish. I will order another bottle.'

'No, honestly, we've got to make an early start tomorrow if we're to get to Delhi.'

'But you will come and have breakfast with me in my home, then?'

'Well, it's very kind of you. We'll just have to see. . . .'

The gallant captain rose somewhat unsteadily to his feet and had to be led back supported on either side. He was adamant, however, that he was still perfectly capable of getting home on his scooter. He let the clutch out, shot forward fifty yards and disappeared abruptly into a gully with a crash that must have roused every cobra from its winter sleep for miles around. Before we could reach him, however, he had remounted and roared off again into the darkness.

We decided to put up the tents after all.

The invitation to breakfast wasn't seriously meant, we all agreed, and even if it was he'd been much too drunk to remember anything about it. Still, perhaps someone ought just to go and check that he'd got home all right. I volunteered.

A line of peasants on their way to a day in the fields directed me to a handsome building surrounded by a verandah and the only one in the village to boast a second storey. Somewhat to my surprise, Captain Bhullar himself greeted me, a model now of sobriety; a few grazes across his knuckles provided the only evidence of anything untoward. He introduced me to his father, a remarkably spry old man who had just returned from a visit to a daughter in Hounslow, his wife, a shy, homely figure, and his two small children, a boy and a girl who regarded me with solemn curiosity. I had great difficulty in explaining why it was that I had come alone, for they had prepared a considerable meal, including an enormous quantity of freshly baked *chapatis*. I couldn't possibly do any sort of justice to them myself, and it was arranged that I should take the remainder back for our lunch. My host produced a bulky photographic album and took me through each stage of his lovingly recorded career: sitting on the lap of the grandfather who had died of the cobra bite, winning the hundred yards at his primary school, receiving his School Certificate, captaining the First Eleven at hockey, passing out of Sandhurst, playing polo for the regiment, leading a troop of Centurions across the Rann of Kutch. With even more pride his daughter showed me her most prized possession, a talking doll; it responded to pressure on its stomach: 'Tell me a story, Mummy', although when squeezed in a somewhat more indelicate part of its anatomy the demand changed to one of 'Let me go into the garden, Mummy'.

I was to have been driven back on the scooter but it refused to start, doubtless due to the abuse it had suffered the previous evening.

For someone who had never ridden on a pillion before balancing a stack of thirty *chapatis*, perhaps it was just as well.

We paused briefly at Amritsar to pay our respects at the Golden Temple, the Mecca of the Sikh religion.

Before entering its precincts, we were obliged to exchange our shoes and socks for squares of orange cloth with which we were expected to cover our heads, although they proved singularly ill-suited for the purpose; Bruce, ever loyal to his Yorkshire origins, succeeded best by tying a knot in each corner. Our first sight of this magnificent shrine, however, at once restored us to a proper decorum; its aura of sanctity and remoteness from its earthly environs was further enhanced by the lake which surrounded it.

A heavy pall of incense hung about its interior, and we had to pick our way with some care between the prostrate bodies of the faithful. John was offered a spoonful from some platters of food which had been placed before the main altar; he reported it to resemble nothing so much as porridge. On the other hand, he confessed that he was much impressed by the absence of idolatry and ritual, and he climbed aloft to compose a paeon to Nanak, who founded the sect in the 15th century.

> Those whom Nanak celebrated in his hymns
> Were warriors and saints, and with these
> He founded a nation within a nation,
> Proud and devoted to the God beyond all forms.
> 'Sow thou a rose to him that soweth thee a thorn,'
> He counselled. 'To thee there is always a rose,
> But to him there is a thorn for evermore.'
> The temple bears him out:
> Built, destroyed by the Afghans, rebuilt
> And then destroyed again, it rose at last

Itself a rose immaculate in marble,
Sheathed in copper overlaid with gold
And set in the great ornamental lake
Amritsar—'The Pool of Nectar'.
Placed on a lower level so that even
The humblest may enter like a king,
Its four doors—one at each point of the compass—
Stand open to admit all pilgrims, regardless
Of belief and origin. 'At the heart
Of the universe white music is blossoming,'
Wrote the poet Kabir, and Nanak too loved music;
The temple is filled with the voices of singers
And musicians chanting one of his hymns
For the thousandth time—they float up to me
In the tower, whose sides are covered with delicate
And jewelled flower patterns of tiny stones
Set in the marble walls.
As I leave, I have a last glimpse of the lake,
Its waters an image of the one
Spoken of in the Upanishads—'The sun-coloured
Being who is beyond the darkness'.
Beside me, a huge smiling ancient murmurs:
'Blessed is Man's going away in the wilderness
And his finding out the way', and I think wryly
How often our little army has gone out
In the wilderness—and lost it.
But in the end it is the words of the other
—Kabir again—that go with me, 'The music
Of the forgetting of sorrows, the music
That transcends all coming in and going forth'.

8   DELHI: WHERE ELSE?

As at Teheran, our arrival in Delhi coincided with the climax of the evening rush hour.

To our relief, however, the camp site was rather more centrally placed than it had been there. The Stock Exchange, a modest building topped by a neon sign flashing 'New Life Corn Flakes', stood opposite. In between, a row of derelict cars lay rusting.

The superintendent required every detail of our passports and vaccination certificates to be written down in triplicate before he would admit us. The charge for three nights worked out at a hundred and fifty-five rupees inclusive of Government Tax, to be paid in advance.

I handed him two sellotaped 100 Rupee notes.

'You think you can cheat me, do you?'

'Cheat you? How?'

'By giving me these fake notes.'

'Of course they aren't fakes.'

'Why then do you stick them together so?'

'Simply because they were torn, that's all.'

'You think I am so stupid as to believe that?'

'Look, you've only got to hold them up to the light and you can see the watermark.'

'I am sorry, you must go now, please.'

'Where to?'

'That is your problem, that is not my problem.'

'You can have the Land-Rover as a deposit.'

'No, it is against all rules and regulations to accept deposits.'

'Will you take dollars, then?'

'Yes, of course, I will take dollars. But if you have dollars, why did you not give them to me first of all?'

'Because they happen to belong to me and not the group.
Understand?'

'Yes, I understand very well, But let me tell you this: if you try to
give those other things you will not succeed, because no one at all
will take them; no one at all in the whole of Delhi.'

And, incredibly, the next morning proved him right: even when
we peeled the offending sellotape off again, they were still rejected
on the grounds that 'the gum could be felt'. They only remedy, we
were informed, lay in the State Reserve Bank.

I was directed to counter Number Seventy-Two, marked
'Exchange of Damaged Notes', and took my place at the end of a
queue which extended almost the entire length of the main hall.

In the next half hour I advanced not more than half a dozen
paces.

'Is it always as slow as this?' I asked my immediate neighbour.

'Yes, always; sometimes even I have been here the whole day
without success. You will just have to be patient, I am afraid.'

'That's easier said than done: I'm only here for a couple of days.'

'Oh dear, that is bad for you: tomorrow the bank will be shut.'

'Shut?'

'Yes: it is a Muslim holiday, you see.'

'But I thought this was a Hindu country.'

'So it is , but we celebrate also the Muslim holidays always.'

'Yes, you would, wouldn't you?' I muttered.

'Allow me to see your notes, and perhaps I can help you.'

'How?'

'Because if they are in not so bad shape you can go to another
counter where you will be quicker.'

I showed them to him, taking care at the same time to keep a
firm grip on them.

'Yes, they are much too good for this counter. You must go to
Counter Number Eighty over there.'

'Are you sure?'

'I am sure, yes. I will show you mine and you will see.' He
reached into his trouser pocket and drew out a few tatty,
discoloured and totally illegible scraps of paper; to my untrained
eyes, they might just as easily have started life as washing powder
coupons.

'I take your point. Thanks very much.'

'You are most welcome.'

The queue at Counter Number Eighty (marked Exchange of Good Notes) was mercifully rather shorter, and in another half an hour I was at its head. To my surprise and relief, all the notes were accepted as genuine; four however, were classified as 'Damaged' rather than 'Good' and I was instructed to return with them to Counter Number Seventy-Two

My acquaintance there signalled to me to rejoin him, much to the annoyance of those behind him. It was going to be touch and go, he explained, whether we would make it before the bank closed.

We did, with five minutes to spare.

John, meanwhile, had been engaged in a similar campaign at the Post Office. At the Poste Restante counter he received a note informing him that a registered letter awaited his collection—not there, however, but at the Central Post Office in the next road.

There he was passed from one tea-drinking clerk to another until in despair he finally forced his way into the main sorting room. An enormous pile of letters stood stacked at one end, and all over the floor men sat cross-legged thumbing through smaller piles and tossing them haphazardly into boxes in the middle; others sat about on tables and chairs in various attitudes of activity, although it was not easy to determine exactly what it was that they were engaged in. Over a desk marked 'Registered Packets' another was slumped sound asleep; a large fly sat preening itself on his nose undisturbed.

John roused him, none too gently. The clerk took a list from a drawer and slowly ran his finger down it.

'Yes, I have it here for you,' he announced.

'Great.'

'But I cannot give it to you now.'

'Why not?'

'Because the supervisor must sign the form first and he is not here.'

'Where is he, then?'

'He has gone home. You must come back the day after tomorrow.'

John made as if to tear out what little hair remained to him.

'But that's absurd: I'm leaving then. You've got to give it to me now.'

'No, I absolutely cannot. I would wish to help you of course, but without the signature of the supervisor I can do nothing. I am so extremely sorry.'

When we met up again at the Camp Site to exchange our experiences, we both decided that we deserved something better and took a room at the Ranjit, one of the city's more modern and prestigious hotels.

The shower was found not to work, but at least the beds didn't collapse in the night.

'Shaver Swish Does the Hat-Trick' a full-page advertisement in the *Times of India* announced at breakfast. 'In the First Test MCC have three wickets to spare and six runs to win. Shaver Swish bowls. Bowled! *"Howzzat!"* the packed crowd roars superfluously. Tea-time . . . and two more wickets to go. As the players go back to the pavilion, a dark-chinned Shaver ponders: "What I need is a super-swift confidence-restoring shave the extra-long handle of the Swish razor and the longer-lasting Swish blades give"–and acts accordingly. The first over after tea yields four runs. Shaver Swish's turn to bowl again. He looks confident . . . bowls . . . *"Howzatt!"* the crowd roars again, "He's out lbw!". The glamorous Ayeesha is similarly excited: "C'mon Shaver Swish!" She screams, "Now's your chance for a hat-trick, darling!" Shaver Swish calls for close field . . . bowls sharply. The batman plays it tamely. Shaver Swish dives forward for a splendid one-handed catch. "It's over!" The crowd roars once more. Ayeesha runs to embrace him: "You won the match for your country, honey!" Thinks Shaver: "You just can't beat the mean who shaves with Swish!"'

On the correspondence page opposite several letters declared that the MCC side should not be received at all: the non-inclusion of Messrs Snow and Boycott reduced it to a Second Eleven side and as such constituted a calculated insult to all cricket-loving Indians. The editor had the last word, however: 'It makes no difference if the team is composed of six tailors from Petticoat Lane and five pastry-cooks from Buckingham Palace, we still all fall over ourselves in the scramble for Test tickets', and proved his point by quoting a report which had them fetching the equivalent of the average monthly salary on the black market. Such fanatical enthusiasm for the game was perhaps only ever matched by that stock caricature of prewar films, the Englishman who strode about

Europe oblivious of the crisis gathering round him and with an eye only for the paper which would give him the latest Test score.

Gorged on eggs and bacon, toast and marmalade, we strolled through the Delhi Gate into the Old City and were immediately swallowed up by a very different world—one on which, if he had ever entered it, the Raj had left no trace, a world of a far earlier age, reminiscent of the Rome of Juvenal.

The two cultures merged uneasily in Connaught Place, formed by three concentric circles of colonnaded shops built perhaps in reproduction of Bath or Cheltenham, but now wearing a less pretentious air. 'The Modern Instrument Company', a sign proclaimed, 'Entrance from the backside'.

I left John deeply immersed in the Buddhist section of the English Language Bookshop and retired to a café with *The Romance of Indian Cricket*. It was, I soon discovered, written in language of a hardly less devotional nature.

'Nisar ran to bowl like a bull at a gate. After a preliminary pawing of the ground, he charged up in eighteen thundering strides. His immense shoulders heaved like billows, his feet in outsize boots pounded at the ground harder and harder, his right hand pistoned up and down purposefully, as he approached the bowling crease—not unlike, to change the simile, an express train at a railway crossing. There was no inhibition in his movements, no holding anything back, no husbanding of his forces. From the first ball he strained nerve and tendon and sinew to achieve his sole and single-minded purpose—that of bowling fast.

'For this purpose, he strove to get his six feet and sixteen stones to attain the maximum momentum at the instant of delivery. He did not leap to a climax like many of his trade, but depended on a dragging right boot to offer him brakage behind the crease. His left arm shot out and up straight as a mast, his small head nearly vanished behind bulging biceps, as his right hand came over in a muscle-stretching sweep. As the bowling arm attained its rapid zenith, Nisar was at the peak and also the finest point of his delivery. After that headlong rush to the wicket, he was now a mighty machine of destruction poised beautifully and perilously on the brink of crisis. The entire impetus of his exertions was transmuted into the propulsive power of that upflung right hand. Then the fingers unloosed the ball and the left foot stamped down and Nisar careered off the pitch in flurry of flannels and dust.'

As I strove to put some sort of picture to the phenomenon thus described, I became aware that I had been joined by a fat Sikh whom I had noticed at another table when I came in. He smiled at me ingratiatingly and pushed a card across the table: Govinda Singh, Phrenologist.

'How are you, my good friend?'

I merely nodded.

' You wish me to tell you your fortune, please?'

I hesitated: it was something that I had always made a point of avoiding in the past.

'Ten rupees only.'

But this was Delhi and perhaps as part of the scene. . . . 'All right, but I only want to hear about the past, not the future. Understand?'

'Yes, yes.'

'You want to be paid now?'

'If you please. You would like also to buy me some mango juice? I work very well on mango juice.'

A waiter had materialised from nowhere and hovered expectantly. I assented.

'Thank you so much, my very good friend. I will work now very well for you, you will see. First of all I will show you these cards and you must choose one thing from each.'

They contained lists of numbers, colours, fruits and flowers. He studied my choices for some time before writing something down on a sheet of paper which he then folded and told me to hold in my left hand. 'Until now your life has been not very happy, yes?

'Maybe.'

'Your father met sudden death, yes?'

'Yes,' (He was killed in the war.)

'About eleven you have been ill for a long time, yes?'

'Yes.' (I was actually ten when I had spent four months in hospital with nephritis.)

'You have loved two ladies before, but it is now broken, yes?'

'Yes.'

'You have a very good friend near here, a J-letter man. He is also bald, yes?'

'Yes.' (It occurred to me that he might have seen and heard me with John in the bookshop but the agility required to have done so and then to have beaten me to the café seemed altogether beyond him.)

'I told you, I work very well for you. Now write down for me on this paper, please, your first name and the day of your birth.' I did so. 'Now show me, please, what you have in your hand.'

They were identical.

Although I had not been looking out for any sleight of hand by which, just possibly, he had engineered this, I had to admit to being impressed.

'Your luck is changing now: no more worry, no more sadness, no more thinking. You wish me to go on? For twenty rupees only I will give you full horoscope.'

'No thanks.'

'You must not worry about money: happiness is more important to you than money. Let me tell you one thing: after seven months another good lady is marrying you.'

'That's going to be rather difficult.'

'A good honest lady, she does not go after other men, only you. A widowed lady loves you; you know widowed lady?'

'No.'

'No, I am sorry, I am wrong. You like lady of the same age, also tall lady. New lady comes not from England, and after marriage you will go with her to foreign country. For five rupees I will tell you where.'

'I'm sorry, I don't want to know.'

'I will tell you her name also: she is an R-letter lady. If you don't believe me, I have here a letter of testimonial from a very famous man in Singapore. Look, I will show you.'

I prepared to leave.

He then produced a faded photograph of an old man in a dhoti. 'He is my guru. Give me a little money please for my guru, for the sake of charity.'

I let him have the small change which the waiter brought.

'Thank you so very much, my very good friend. Think of me when your good luck comes.' He leant forward a little and whispered: 'Tell me, when did you last have sexual intercourse?'

'You ought to be able to tell me that.'

'You like Hindu ladies? I know very nice Hindu lady, one hundred rupees only. . . .'

Eschewing such a delightful prospect, I rejoined the others for an evening's entertainment at the Apollo circus.

Long queues had already formed for the cheaper seats, and we soon decided to try for the Dress Circle at five rupees each. Half a dozen people were clustered about the grille, and it was some time before we realised that there was no one on its other side. After persistent enquiries at the main entrance, we managed to establish that there were in fact still seats available and were led round behind the elephants' quarters to a hut where a man sat gluing government tax stamps on individual tickets by the light of a paraffin lamp. Only with extreme reluctance could he be persuaded to interrupt this labour of love long enough to issue us with some of them.

In spite of the queues, the tent was no more than a quarter full when the performance began; the 'Dress Circle' was distinguished from the cheaper seats only by its proximity to the ring. The opening act provided a good indication of what was to come: a steel-helmeted figure appeared at the wheel of a jeep, roared up a ramp with the intention of launching himself across a gap of perhaps five yards, thought better of it at the last second and toppled ignominiously into it. He was followed by a troupe of clowns and a juggler who needed at least three attempts to pull off the simplest trick; hard as they tried, his companions' antics could not divert us from his embarrassment. The level of competence varied in inverse proportion to the age of the performers: the panache and versatility of the pair of ten-year-old acrobats made a rather better impression than did a team of portly trapezists and tightrope-walkers, whose turns were as brief as they were unambitious. The animals—elephants, lions, horses—were little more than paraded round the ring, and the tiger, a creature of almost comical docility, was manoeuvred about the cage by ropes held from the outside. The star performer was undoubtedly a giant of a man in a leopard skin who swallowed several gallons of water containing a number of goldfish and then regurgitated them intact, but even this feat owed rather more to a physical abnormality than any acquired skill. The evening was brought to a fitting close by the ejection of the hero in the helmet from a cannon, followed after a considerable interval by a report—but by then the audience, who had sat throughout in a stoical silence, was already making for the exit.

When John and I got back to the Ranjit, we were not surprised to find that the lift too was now out of order.

> After an age of wandering
> We came to a land, where evenings
> Are like pearl, and the rivers
> Are like inland seas.
> Then this city, where the legendary Pandavas
> Ruled millenia ago, and whose glory
> Has not yet faded. Nearby, a sacred cow
> Sleeps on the steps of the theatre
> Until the crowd arrives—perhaps
> It is one who was once human, before the gods
> Changed its form—we do not know
> And do not ask. We stand drinking the cool juice
> Of strange fruits, leaning against the stall
> Of our friend Bandhulla Khan.
> He bobs and talks to us, teaching us
> To count in Hindhi, and telling us in mime
> Of his four fine sons, whom we know will be
> As brave and fine as Rama himself,
> And when we understand, he gives us
> One of his amazing smiles, and from his secret store
> More of the coloured, bubbling ambrosia.
> Afterwards, we eat, then full of good rice,
> Dal and hot lamb curry, we return, belching
> Like bedouins to our deserted tents.
> Far off in the peaceful gardens across the city
> The tiny squirrels still play on the lawns
> Beneath the great tower of Qutub Minar
> While the birds go to rest
> And the solitary piper by the roadside
> Watches his serpents dance
> Till they are shadows.

9   PARADISE LOST

A boat-builder from the Norfolk Broads, called Richard, had meanwhile flown in to join us. Tall and lean, he had a purposeful look about him, as if he meant to walk the pants off the rest of us; he talked ominously of previous treks in the Dolomites.

The prospect of travelling twelve in the Land-Rover persuaded me to look into the possibility of other means of transport, however temporary. After an exhaustive study of the train timetables, I worked it out that I could catch a morning train to Agra, have the rest of the day at the Taj Mahal, take a sleeper to Benares and arrive there at almost exactly the same time as the Land-Rover. The Tourist Office warned me that they were not altogether reliable, being subject to day-to-day alterations without notice. It still seemed a risk worth taking.

Bruce and Heather also arrived at the same decision, as eventually did John after another sortie on the Post Office. This time he had succeeded in extracting his letter, only to find that it contained some postal orders from his well-meaning grandmother which were unencashable anywhere outside the British Isles.

The station presented a scene of utter confusion. Each of the forty-odd counters in the main booking hall was besieged by a milling semicircle of applicants; on the wall above them a faded poster, a relic of the Raj, extolling the advantages of 'getting into the Q habit' provided a touch of irony. To confound us further, they were classified not according to their respective destinations but by sub-divisions of the railway system: there was nothing to tell us whether Agra fell within the domain of the Northern Railway, the North-Eastern Railway, the Central Railway or the District Railway, and everyone we asked was much too intent on the struggle for their own ticket to answer us. The only way of resolving the problem was for the four of us to take one each.

After battling my way to the front I was able to establish that I was at the right one. Even now, however, I was still a long way from my goal: as soon as one person withdrew with his ticket, half a dozen hands would shoot into the vacant hole in the grille to confront the bewildered clerk. Time was getting short, and in the end I adopted the drastic tactic of thrusting my arm through right up to the shoulder, to the painful exclusion of all my competitors. It worked, although I had to abandon any idea of booking places on the sleeper to Benares.

The 'Taj Express' was already standing at the platform, headed by a magnificent steam engine; its driver was lovingly polishing one of its copper pipes. Behind it, the carriages were being treated with rather less respect by the hundreds of people fighting to get aboard; men charged at the doors holding their baggage in front of them as battering rams, and if that failed they scrambled in through the windows and shouted at their families to hand it up to them. After walking more than half the length of the train we began to think that we would have to take the same route; then out of the blue we came to an empty doorway and a compartment occupied only by a middle-aged couple. We rapidly established ourselves in it. The husband explained the mystery: it was officially reserved for the use of women, but they were allowed to invite their menfolk to join them if they so wished; Heather's presence therefore made it all right for us to stay. When the train eventually pulled out, disappointed passengers still lined the platform several rows deep; we could hardly believe our luck. John began to celebrate it on his flute. My admiration for his skill on this particular instrument was something less than total, and anyway having several days to get up in my diary, I took the excuse to move into the next compartment. Its sole occupant stood looking out of the window. Although she was not quite upright, I could tell that she was unusually tall, perhaps even six-foot; her black, glossy hair reached almost to her waist and she wore a Western-style outfit of sweater and trousers which did her lissom figure better justice than a sari would have done. When she turned, I was still more agreeably surprised, for her features were quite as perfect as the rest of her; the description 'doe-like' would not begin to convey the depth of tenderness and feeling which her eyes expressed. She was, without exaggeration (if such a claim can ever be made in these matters), the loveliest creature that I had ever seen.

She smiled, and I was instantly bewitched. I just managed to stutter some banality about the weather and to my joy she motioned me to sit beside her. Her father, she told me, was a professor at Simla University, and she herself had a degree in English Literature; she had trained as an air hostess but had now switched to the stage; her name was Madhu. The conversation moved on to our common interest and we found that our tastes coincided: we both preferred Smollett to Fielding, Dickens to Scott, Trollope to Hardy, Galsworthy to Forster, Fitzgerald to Hemingway, Waugh to Greene. Surely no three hours have ever passed more quickly on Indian Railways, nor any of its passengers been so sorry to reach his destination. I suggested that we exchanged addresses, but reluctantly had to agree with her that there was really little point and instead left her with a more appropriate memento—my paperback copy of *A Handful of Dust.*

The others greeted my reappearance with massive ribaldry, but for the moment I was deaf to anything except the memory of her lilting voice. We deposited our bags at the Left Luggage Office and decided that we could afford a taxi for the four-mile journey to the Taj Mahal.

For the second time that day I was completely bowled over. Its beauty lay far beyond the compass of any words—or rather, of any words of mine; the chattering droves of tourists could not detract from it, nor even the fact that the fountains were out of order. I could only watch and wonder as the dazzling white of its marble turned to a delicate primrose, then finally at sunset to an incandescent gold. On the mud flats of the River Yamuna below men crouched patiently washing their clothes in the still waters; from time to time a leaky punt slid lazily across.

John also confessed himself lost for words: the advance publicity had already said everything that there was to say.

As if to compensate us for the absence of the fountains, we were told that the gates would be open until midnight in honour of the full moon. Our train for Benares left at ten; a quick curry at the nearest restaurant gave us another hour and a half.

I made another slow circuit on my own before settling down against the trunk of a eucalyptus tree in one of the less frequented corners of the grounds. As the moon climbed higher into the silver sky the whole building took on an ethereal quality until it seemed to rise with it from its earthly foundations. Then gradually earlier memories of the day began to impinge on my enchantment, and it became no longer the monument of Shah Jahan to his wife, but mine to Madhu, so perfectly did they match each other. If only she was with me now. . . .

My reverie was broken by someone tripping over my legs. I looked at my watch. Five past nine: the others would be waiting for me at the entrance. I rejoined them and turned for one last look. Suddenly I realised that I had forgotten my diary and zip folder containing, amongst other things, my passport and wallet. I ran back to the eucalyptus tree. They were no longer there.

Crisis.

The wallet wasn't so important—I had learnt my lesson in Persia and left most of my money in the Land-Rover's locker—or even the diary with its sixty pages of notes, but the passport. . .

Nor had they been handed in at the gate. The others generously volunteered to stay on and help in the search, but I told them that such a thing was out of the question: it was bad enough having one of the party adrift, let alone four. If I could find my things that night I would catch them up at Benares; if I couldn't, I would just have to make my own way to Kathmandu by whatever means. Bruce gave me a hundred rupees, and we exchanged sombre farewells.

I didn't find them that night, even with the help of some of the guides and the local police. By now all the taxis had departed; only a single rickshaw, powered by quite a young boy, remained to take me back to the town. Some of the inclines were too much for him, and he was obliged to get off and push; when he did get up speed, the rush of cold air caused me to shiver convulsively. The journey took over half an hour, by which time all the hotels worthy of the name were found to be shut. Eventually we ended up at a dosshouse in the slum quarter. After hammering on the door until it threatened to come away from its rusty hinges, an ill-kempt, betel-chewing proprietor appeared with a candle and spat copiously about him as we negotiated. He led me up a flight of stairs and over several bodies laid out on the open balcony to a room which was just wide enough to accommodate two hardboard beds (a notice on the back of the door certified it as being sixty foot square); for this I was charged an extortionate eight rupees. With it came one filthy blanket; squadrons of mosquitoes, but no nets; an overpowering stench of sewage and immediately below, the intermittent clatter of shunting trains.

There was no hope of sleep; between warding off the mosquitoes, I could only lie and reflect on the fickleness of Fate which had raised me so high and brought me so low in the space of a single day.

10 PASSPORT REGAINED

To rise at dawn was, for once, a pleasure rather than an ordeal, and in my haste to escape I trod hard on one of my fellow guests. He blinked at me for a few moments, then with a sudden shriek of terror pulled the blanket back over his head. He had every excuse for thinking me a figure of nightmare, I conceded.

After another fruitless three hours at the Taj I reported to the police station. A sergeant took down my statement in rudimentary English, then transcribed it laboriously into Urdu three times over. Having signed each copy I was taken before the superintendent, who was sunning himself on the verandah, drinking tea.

'Oh my goodness me, this is very bad for you,' he said, clicking the end of his baton against his teeth.

'You don't give me much chance of getting it back, you mean?

'I should say not indeed. This place is literally bursting with thieves and such people; in the whole of India you will not find a worse place than this. Of course my men will do their utmost for you, but I cannot give you hope.'

'What do you think I ought to do, then?'

'If you ask me honestly, I advise you to speak to your embassy in Delhi, and they will tell you what you must do'

'Can I use your telephone?'

'I am so very sorry, but it is not working now. If you go to the Post Office in Agra town they will be able to help you, I am sure.'

'Thanks.'

However, I decided that I'd had enough of Indian officialdom for the moment and made instead for the Clark Shiraz International Hotel. I was put through without difficulty and instructed to return immediately to Delhi and apply for a new passport. Wouldn't it be worth waiting at Agra another day in case it turned up? No; I ought to realise that a British passport could fetch anything up to £500 on the black market.

I did what I was told.

It was not until I was back at the Left Luggage Office that another appalling thought struck me: all our baggage had been entered on the same ticket, which of course Bruce had taken with him, and without it I saw no prospect whatever of retrieving my kitbag.

I explained to the attendant exactly what had happened.

'What is your name, please?'

'Montgomery.'

'You are seven feet high, yes?'

'Well, not quite; six and a bit.'

'And you weigh thirteen stones, is that correct?'

'More or less.'

'I am your very good friend, then.'

'Oh, really?'

'Yes, indeed. If you will just sign your name here in the book, I will go and get your bag for you.'

Mystified but highly relieved, I hurried away with it before he could change his mind.

By the time I reached Delhi, the embassy had shut for the day. My hundred rupees were down now to twenty, which condemned me to a supper of rice (two rupees) and a night at the Camp Site (five). I shared a marquee with a group of French hippies, and astonished them by declining their offer of a 'joint'.

The next morning I presented myself punctually at the embassy's opening time of ten o'clock. The process of applying for a new passport proved straight-forward enough, involving no more than providing evidence of the loss of the old one (the sergeant's Urdu was accepted), supplying a photograph and filling in a form. These were, however, two drawbacks. Firstly, it would take three days for confirmation to be received from London, which meant that only a flight would get me to Kathmandu in time to meet up with the others; and secondly, the cost of something like £10 was payable in advance. I pointed out that my present resources amounted to no more than thirteen rupees; wasn't there an emergency fund to deal with this sort of situation? The Passport Secretary took a battered cigarette tin from his desk and turned it upside down; out fell two single rupee coins. The fund was maintained entirely from voluntary contributions, he explained. Well then, couldn't somebody in the embassy lend me the money just for the three days? No, that wasn't the done thing at all; my best plan was to go to National & Grindlays and try to arrange a loan there through my own bank. Of course, I was welcome to the two rupees if they would help towards my rickshaw fare. . . .

I preferred to walk.

At the bank I received another setback: they too would require three days in which to exchange telegrams. I protested that National & Grindlay's was a subsidiary of my own bank, so that all they had to do was to telephone headquarters. No longer, I was informed: the Indian government had nationalised all banks earlier in the year. As a last resort I tried the manager of the Ranjit. Yes, he remembered me; however, he was very sorry, he would like to help of course, but the hotel being government-owned. . . .

I trudged back to the embassy, wondering how on earth I was going to survive for three days on thirteen rupees.

I was surprised to see the Passport Secretary's impassive features break into a smile. 'I have some good news for you,' he said.

What could it be? Had someone been so moved by my plight as to add another rupee to the emergency fund?

'I've got your things here.' He held out my folder.

I stared at it, speechless.

'Some Indian fellow brought it in a few minutes ago. Apparently he was on his way from Bangalore to stay with relatives in Delhi when he stopped at the Taj for the full moon. And if you're wondering why he brought it here instead of handing it into the local police, the answer probably is that he knows them rather better than you do. He's name's Shashi Kumar; he left his address in case you might like to get in touch with him.'

I laid the folder on the desk and went slowly through its contents. Everything was just as I had left it: my passport, my wallet with its one hundred and twenty rupees, my bank credit card, my diary.

Mister Shashi Kumar, I regret that I never did manage to contact you that day (although I did write you a letter), but should you ever read this, you will know just how deeply I stand in your debt: you saved me firstly, the combined cost of a new passport and a flight to Kathmandu; secondly, the prospect of living off the streets of Delhi for three days; thirdly and perhaps most important, the labour of getting up those first sixty pages of notes from memory. Words cannot express my gratitude; let me tell you that even today I still finger my passport every so often to satisfy myself that I wasn't the victim of some cruel mirage, so utterly was I convinced that I would never see it again.

At the Tourist Office I learnt that I could catch a mail train to Lucknow at ten o'clock that night and after two more changes (at Muzaffarpur and Sagauli respectively) be at Raxaul on the Nepalese border thirty-three hours later; if the others had preceded me, I could then catch a bus which would get me to Kathmandu the same day. The third-class fare cost sixty-one rupees, the bus another twenty-five; I calculated that I could just afford an additional twenty for a second-class sleeper as far as Lucknow.

Obtaining the appropriate ticket was, I soon discovered, quite another matter. Counter 17 refused to issue a second-class ticket without a sleeper ticket; Counter 30 refused to issue a sleeper ticket without a reservation; Counter 20 refused to issue a reservation for the unanswerable reason that there weren't any left. It came as something of a surprise, therefore, when I was able to buy a third-class ticket at Counter 38 without being referred to yet another counter. I then remembered that the Tourist Office had told me that sleeper reservations could also be made in the Railway Headquarters building. It seemed worth trying, even though it did lie on the opposite side of the city.

Thousands of bicycles stood neatly racked in its forecourt. Inside I could see rows of clerks perched on high stools poring over ledgers. I was directed down a long corridor to a small room marked 'Requisitions for Reservations Tourists Only'. The official behind its single table assured me that it was far too late to make any reservations for that night. I filled in an application form nonetheless, then made such a nuisance of myself that he finally lost patience and signed it.

Thus armed, I returned to the station. The clerk at Counter 20 appeared slightly more impressed, but he still refused to issue a reservation without a sleeper ticket from Counter 30, who refused to issue one without a second-class ticket from Counter 17—thus exactly reversing the previous cycle. As I began handing over the money, it suddenly occurred to me that I would not have enough until I was refunded for my third-class ticket. Counter 38, however, required written authority from Counter 22 before he would do so, and this new star in the firmament announced that he was just off for his tea-break. . . .

It was not until shortly after eight o'clock, seven hours after I had first arrived, that I had the three tickets in my hand.

I retrieved my kitbag from the camp site, snatched another bowl of rice and was back at the station in time for the arrival of the Lucknow Mail. It was just as well that I was, for no sooner had I established myself on my sleeper than two others arrived to claim it. In vain I pointed out to them that the numbers on their tickets referred to those on the seats rather than the sleepers; they resolved the argument by sitting on me, a position which they maintained throughout the night. Two more then settled down on the floor immediately beneath me; when they weren't smoking foul-smelling cheroots, they snored. Being right on the end of the line, I also suffered the additional handicap of being next to both the door and the lavatory. In short, I might just as well have saved myself all that trouble and stayed in the third-class—at least I'd have been twenty rupees better off. As it was, I felt able to spend no more than two rupees on a breakfast of toast and coffee at the Lucknow station restaurant, and a further rupee on six small bananas to last me the rest of the day.

According to the Tourist Office the Muzaffarpur train was due to leave at 9.20; according to the station timetable, 10.45. In fact it left at 11.25. By this time fifteen bodies had crowded into my compartment. Opposite me sat a mother and her four children. She held the youngest at her breast and did what she could at the same time to keep the others under control. The eldest, a particularly fractious girl, frequently lashed out at her mother who replied in kind, to the noisy consternation of the baby. By contrast four or five hens emprisoned in a wicker basket, their legs trussed, maintained a commendable silence. Beside me was ranged an even larger family, which included both parents and grandparents. The children, all six of them, were dispatched to the luggage rack, and for the next twelve hours two pairs of bare, grubby feet dangled not six inches in front of my nose. At the first stop still more tried to force their way in and were repulsed—with one exception, a man of maniacal aspect and persistence who swung himself up on to the other rack and squeezed himself horizontally into the few inches that still remained between baggage and ceiling, from where he scowled down at the rest of us like an outraged monkey.

The heat of the afternoon did nothing to improve conditions. A trickle of filthy water from a leaking basin (or something worse) further down the corridor began to seep into the compartment. When it had absorbed most of the dust and detritus on the floor the fractious girl unpeeled a banana, dropped it into the puddle, rolled it around until it was thoroughly soaked—then ate it. I dared not look at her again, and kept my eyes shut tight for the rest of the journey. It brought me no nearer sleep, however: the tea-vendors at every station with their ear-splitting bleat of '*chai, chai, chai*' saw to that.

We were due to reach Muzaffarpur shortly before midnight. At the last station before it we jerked in and out of the platform several times before coming to a standstill again. The engine worked up a fine rage on its hooter. People began to disembark. I asked a porter what was happening and was told that there had been an accident on the line ahead; I would have to transfer to another train. The news caused pandemonium in the compartment, and as we fought to extricate ourselves the train suddenly began to reverse out of the station in earnest. I was just able to pile out of it in time. No so the two families: they and a considerable proportion of the other passengers disappeared into the night, never to be seen again. No one showed the least concern for their fate, and for all I know, they may still be rotting against the buffers of some remote branch line.

The confusion of those on the platform was hardly less: no one, least of all any of the railway staff, had the slightest idea of when a relief train might arrive. When it did, an hour later, it drew in on the far side of the station, provoking a wild stampede across the intervening rails. It had only four carriages compared with the eleven of the original train, and these were found to be already well filled. What happened next would not have looked out of place among the battle honours of a regiment of Japanese storm-troopers. Wave after wave of humanity threw itself at the doors, and a detachment of soldiers was hastily called out to defend the single First Class carriage, bayonets at the ready. No sooner had I gained a foothold on the bottom step than I was dragged off it from behind. This happened twice more. Finally I grabbed hold of a large sack which three men were struggling to haul aboard and allowed myself to be pulled in after it. Inside, the battle grew still more intense. I was propelled further and further along the corridor by the weight of those still pouring in behind me until I was brought up against the irresistible force of those moving up from the other end. Up to that point I had had the alternative of turning off into a compartment, although none had seemed to offer any better prospect; now I had as much room for manoeuvre as a potted shrimp, and if I had tried to sit I would certainly have been trampled to death. Those with children in tow had wisely stood aside from the fray; when they saw that there was no possibility of finding any room for them themselves, they handed them up through the windows to be passed over the heads of those in the corridor and deposited on the luggage racks before taking to the roof. I could still hear them padding about above me when the train eventually moved off.

For the next two hours it was all I could do to breathe. My immediate neighbours were four gnarled old men all armed with long sticks which caught me painfully in the ribs every time I exhaled. A continuous retching and spitting made their company still less agreeable: nobody in this world retches and spits quite so offensively as an old Indian.

We made several more unscheduled stops. One of them was preceded by such a hubbub on the roof that I was led to suppose that someone had fallen off. At Muzaffarpur very few of my fellow passengers were seen to disembark, and I was obliged to climb out through the window—only to find that this was the train that was due to take me to Degauli. When I attempted to board it again by the same route the old men closed ranks and fended me off with their sticks, forcing me to do battle once more at the door. I could get no further than the top step, and passed the next three hours in this precarious position. I had only the cold to thank for keeping me awake.

Dawn was just breaking as we reached Dagauli. The connecting train was already waiting for us and, even more surprisingly, arrived at Raxaul at exactly the time predicted by the Tourist Office—7.15 am.

If in the past week I had done no more than scratch at India's surface, her railway system was one area in which I now felt able to claim the right to be excused from digging any deeper.

At the customs house, a single-room affair tucked away unannounced beside a hotel, I asked to be allowed to inspect the Vehicle Exit Record Book; there was no mention of the Land-Rover.

I adjourned to the hotel next door and established myself by the front window of its restaurant for the day's vigil.

Perhaps half a dozen vehicles passed through that morning, none of them a Land-Rover. Without exception, they drove straight past and were referred back again at the border. The only travellers to arrive in the opposite direction were a large party of migratory Tibetans who were on their way down from the hills to spend the winter in a community centre set up for their compatriots. They came on foot and carried all their possessions with them, including great balls of goat's cheese; the women, children slung across their backs and cooking utensils dangling from their waists, made an especially picturesque sight.

I reached for my camera, but before I could do so much as to raise it to my eye the customs official darted out of his room waving his arms excitedly.

'You must not do that here, please.'

'Why not?'

'Because it is absolutely forbidden to make photographs here.'

'Yes, but why?'

'Because this is a situation of strategical importance.'

'You're joking, of course.'

'No, I am not at all joking. Please will you do what I tell you before you oblige me to call the police.'

Remembering that he still had to clear me, I desisted from further argument and returned to my post.

By mid-afternoon I could stand the shrill sing-song of the cookboy's transistor no longer, and went for a walk down the line of tinker's hovels that constituted the town's main street.

Crowds of men drifted from one to another, sadly surveying their shoddy wares; nothing ever changed hands. A dilapidated lorry came lurching over the potholes, its horn blaring; they parted and closed in again silently behind it. Every few yards wild-eyed tonga drivers implored me to avail myself of the services of their cadaverous animals. The outstretched hands of beggar women tugged repeatedly at my clothes. Naked children squatted excreting in the roadside dust. In the palm trees above vultures squabbled raucously for points of vantage.

If the world comes to a dead-end anywhere, it is surely at Raxaul.

The customs house closed at six, leaving me to negotiate terms for the night with the proprietor of the hotel. He expressed himself quite happy to give me credit when I explained that the Land-Rover would be arriving the next day with my money, and under this arrangement I was able to take my first square meal for four days.

I slept uninterruptedly for twelve hours; not even the mosquitoes could disturb me, although I was later to wish that they had done so. There had been some rain overnight, giving Raxaul a still more dismal appearance.

At breakfast I fell into conversation with an Indian who was employed by Toyota to deliver cars from Calcutta to Kathmandu. He offered to give me a lift, and I accepted: nothing else was going to get me there as comfortably. However, when I told the proprietor to present my bill to Fabian on his arrival, he refused to allow me to leave before it had been paid. I recounted the terms of our agreement the previous evening, but in vain; he was adamant.

I found out later that he was the local Congress Party boss.

My new friend's lurid accounts of the frequent pile-ups he had come across on his way forced me to anxious calculations: if the Land-Rover had left Benares, three hundred and fifty miles away, at noon on Thursday and it was now Sunday morning. . . .

Then, quite suddenly, there it was outside, dripping with mud.

As reunions went, it was unemotional. No, they hadn't really been worried about me; merely grateful for the extra space. No, I hadn't missed much: the burning ghats at Benares were really rather morbid. Oh yes, there had been a bit of a row over whether they should visit Bhudgaia, the scene of Buddha's enlightenment, and John had almost come to blows with one of his opponents; but that was about all, really.

Bruce explained for me the mystery of my reception at the Agra Left Luggage Office. On producing the ticket, he had given the attendant a detailed account of my misadventure and asked him to keep my kitbag until I arrived to claim it.

'No, it is impossible for me to do that,' the other had replied flatly.

'Why?'

'Because how can I know this person?'

'Well, his name's Montgomery, he's got brownish hair and blue eyes, weighs thirteen stone and stands about seven feet high.'

'But there are many such people in this country.'

'You're telling me there are seven-foot giants tramping all over India? Give over, mate.'

'And even if he is genuine, how do I know that you are genuine?'

The absurdity of the question had finally brought Bruce to the boil. 'Because my name's down there on the bloody ticket, you great twit.'

'You say that is your name, but how can I know if you are telling me the truth?'

'Look, that's my name and that's my property, and if you don't get it for me I'm going to get it myself, see?'

'Please, you cannot do such a thing. I am an official of the Indian Government and therefore I am inviolable.'

'Are you really?' John, foreseeing disaster, had interposed, and immediately launched himself into a long, rambling panegyric of the Indian Civil Service. It had had the desired effect, for the attendant had eventually agreed to release all the bags on condition that mine was re-entered on a fresh ticket and my description written down on the back of it.

As they waited for the train Heather had prudently asked a porter for the whereabouts of the lavatory and had met with the astonishing reply: 'I am so sorry, I am very regrettable to tell you that that train has been delayed; it will not now be arriving until. . . .'

11 KATHMANDU: LAND OF NOD

The bustle and squalor of India fell away behind us as we climbed tortuously through tropical forests to a pass of over eight thousand feet. The road, the first to link Nepal with the outside world, had been open for less than twenty years, although (as we learnt from a near-fatal encounter on a hairpin bend) this had been long enough for Coca Cola Inc. to add another outpost to its empire.

After a night in a *chaie khana* just short of the top we descended again to Kathmandu. My first impression of it did not at all conform to the mountainside capital of my imagination; instead, it sprawled untidily from the centre of a flat, featureless plain.

We installed ourselves in the annexe of the Snow View Hotel, itself a misnomer: when the Himalayas were visible at all through the heat haze, they were pushed into the far background by ranges of intervening hills. John and I shared a room enlivened by the scampering of mice in the ceiling, but at eight rupees a head for four nights we could hardly expect the company of less. I opened the door of what I took to be a cupboard and found a dark, narrow passage. At the end of it lay a bath, the monumental creation of the unlikely combination of Messrs Pontifex and Emanuel, London W1. Its pair of splendid brass taps refused to yield any water, however, and further investigation proved them to be unconnected to any pipes. It was a cruel trick to play on someone who had spent the last six weeks in a Land-Rover.

The hotel proper had a passé, post-colonial air about it. Numerous white-coated servants padded along its corridors conveying a quiet sense of purpose, but its only residents as far as I could discover were an elderly American couple who had clearly not come for the mountain air, still less the hashish. The reading room provided for their enjoyment a pile of dog-eared *Life* magazines, a pair of drooping potted palms and an electric fire which gave off some dazzling sparks but no heat.

To be charitable, the lack of patronage might also have had something to do with its position on the outskirts of the town.

'I've just discovered a rather nasty crack in the top of my horn.' John announced after a preliminary survey of his equipment. 'You don't know where I can find a blacksmith or somebody who could put a band round it, do you, Fabian?'

'God, don't tell me you're taking that thing on the trek with you.'

'Yes, of course I am. Besides, it'll come in pretty useful if I ever get lost.'

'You get lost, John? I don't believe it.'

'Well, you never know. Anyway, when's the Land-Rover going into town?'

'It's not.'

'Oh, why's that?'

'One, because petrol costs something like twenty rupees a gallon here; two, because it's just done seven thousand miles and I reckon it deserves a rest; and three, you've got a few miles ahead of you now so you might as well start getting used to the idea of walking. All right?'

'If you say so.'

'Or if that's going to be too much of a strain for you, you can always hire a bike from the hotel.'

Presently nine cyclists set out in a wobbling column. We were soon feeling more confident, however, for bicycles, with or without rickshaws attached, were very much the dominant mode of transport; ridden as many as six abreast, they effectively dictated the pace of the few cars that there were, and generally ignored the even rarer sets of traffic lights.

We called first at the Post Office to collect our mail. The building's functional facade flattered to deceive, for its interior was the setting for the same confusion that had confronted us at the Delhi Railway Station, enacted this time on a rather more limited stage. Forty or fifty tourists surged round the Poste Restante counter shouting transatlantic obscenities, oblivious of the line of natives struggling to deliver parcels to the adjacent counter. With a fine show of disdain the clerk took the passports thrust at him through and over the grille one at a time, drew a pile of letters from the appropriate pigeon-hole and thumbed slowly through it. We soon decided that there were better ways of spending our time.

The town came over as a curious hybrid of East and West, of ancient and modern, but without the violent, comical contrasts of, say, Kabul, and as such it seemed to lack the character of either; it was almost as if it was still making up its mind which it wanted to be. The newer sector was dominated by the Royal Bank of Nepal; unfortunately, as is the case with banks the world over, its bulk was not matched by its architectural merits. A retired Gurkha guarded its doors with a venerable shotgun. In the same street respective ideologies glowered at each other from the windows of the American Cultural Center, the Soviet-Nepalese Library and the House of Friendship of the People's Republic of China, politely ignored by the amiable citizenry. The British Council lay further out, aloof from such vulgar competition; it was chiefly valuable for its supply of fortnight-old copies of *The Times* (the *Rising Nepal* was printed daily, but it did not constitute much of a link with the outside world: its front page that day was given over to the report of a tiger's momentary escape from the Zoo). Opposite stood the Royal Hotel, once the starting point of all Everest expeditions but now a sorry picture of decay. The story was that its owner, Boris, a Russian ex-ballet dancer, had closed it down in order to concentrate his energies on his other venture, the Yak and Yeti Restaurant; 'you must go and have a meal there', everyone in the Council said, but no one could actually tell us where it was. Another near neighbour was the newly built Royal Palace; it was not, however, a very imposing structure, and anywhere else it would have passed as the site of a trade fair. Immediately outside its gates a portly cow sat in the road, chewing its cud contentedly.

In the old quarter, a quaint network of narrow alleys, bicycles as well as cars gave grudging precedence to carts, barrows and pedestrians. The larger intersections were marked by plain, white-washed *stupas* (Buddhist shrines), and in the complex of pagodas towards its western end even John found few individual features to excite him. The dark, low-lintelled shops fell almost exclusively into three categories—grocers, ironmongers, haber-dashers—and within each category offered the same limited range of goods. Fruit and vegetables were laid out on straw mats in the streets; they were measured in hand-held scales, a method calculated to baffle the most intimate knowledge of Nepalese avoirdupois. Hashish was openly advertised for sale, but there was no sign of the sinister associations given to the fact in the West; if any foreigners had dropped dead in the streets of Kathmandu, it was much easier to suppose that they had fallen victim to the all-pervasive lethargy of the place and had simply given up the ghost.

The following day brought contradiction: paper streamers fluttered from every lamp-post; long columns of bicycles converged on the central parade ground; children ran beside them waving flags; lorries got up as floats blundered about blindly; the imperturbable cow had moved on

I looked to the *Rising Nepal* for an explanation. I was not disappointed.

'Prime Minister appeals all to celebrate auspicious occasion of His Majesty King Birendra's birthday with enthusiasm' ran the main headline. The editor could hardly be accused of ignoring this injunction, for other headlines included 'HM Birendra: a profile in courage', 'King Birendra and the concept of development', 'Crown's leadership lauded'; 'The personality of HM Birendra,' 'Royal leadership in Education', 'The King and the People'. An article entitled 'a moment in Eton' seemed to promise some variation on the theme, and even Old Etonians may bear with me if I quote it at some length.

'Spring 1960. We were discussing our programme with the Director-General of British Central Office of Information and his colleagues at the Foreign Office. We had arrived London the day before as a four-member delegation to tour the United Kingdom at the invitation of Her Britannic Majesty's Government. The team was composed of two political persons, a Royal Army Officer and myself.

The British officials were very eager to ensure our complete satisfaction, so much so that one of them quietly remarked to me "In general, this programme of inviting foreign guests ends up in sheer wastage of public funds; if it could be ensured that we always receive guests like you, then the sweat of the tax-payers could be deemed to have been put to good use". After a discussion lasting longer than was customary, the programme was about finalized. There still remained one important gap. To me it was totally unthinkable that I should visit England and return home without paying due respects to His Majesty King Birendra (then His Royal Highness The Crown Prince) who was studying at Eton. To my mind that was the most important point, not only from the angle of personal loyalty and reverence: I had the feeling that the imperatives of the time demanded that at least the decision-making section of the British Government, if not the whole of the British Public opinion, be exposed to the realities of the then political situation and the inner springs of the recently promulgated Constitution of the Kingdom of Nepal. It could not be resolved on the spot. Subsequently when we were received by Mr. Harold MacMillan who was then the British Prime Minister, we did our best to acquaint him with all those things in their proper perspective.

In the end it was agreed to include the visit only on approval by His Royal Highness. Suppose the approval was withheld, what then? Would it be right to try a more direct approach? But how? Till then I had never had an opportunity to be received in audience by His Royal Highness. What reasonable or possible ground could I think up for making a direct approach? As I walked down the big stone-paved staircase of the Foreign Office I was absorbed in an inward debate of this kind. I tried to ease my burden a little. In the evening I put a call through to the Royal Nepalese Ambassador. Unfortunately, however, I found that he was not in a position to give me a definite advice.

In almost all countries administration is viewed as synonymous with dilatoriness. The UK is not perhaps an exception. But I realized that the British administration had the ability to grasp full well the state of mind and the sense of urgency in others when an official of the Central Office of Information informed me over the phone that His Royal Highness had expressed his willingness to see us. What a privilege!

On the appointed day when we reached Eton an assistant headmaster, waiting to receive us, said after the exchange of the usual formalities: "Would you prefer to go round the premises first and see His Royal Highness later or would you prefer it the other way round? For, as I've been informed by the Prince, he has to take part in a football match and he can receive you only before or after the match." Naturally, we chose to see His Royal Highness first.

When, escorted by the assistant headmaster, we arrived at the door of one of the rooms in the hostel, His Majesty was busy cleaning a pair of boots which he was to wear at the football match. "Look, I can't even offer a couple of chairs for you to sit down." His Majesty observed with a simplicity and grace natural to a student, as he came out into the corridor. In all deference we introduced ourselves and when my turn came, His Majesty inquired, "You are the Director of Nepal Radio, I suppose." At this it was certainly my weakness that I felt an upsurge of pride in me. His Majesty, of course, loves and cares for us all in equal measure. His Majesty briefly spoke about Nepal and some of the points in England and in Eton which we should on no account miss. We, on our part, laid before His Majesty such information as we deemed fit for communication to the Royalty.

Somewhere down the passageway a bell rang. That was the signal for proceeding to the playing-field. His Majesty turned to us and remarked, "Oh, It's time to go. Sorry I couldn't have time to offer some tea. I don't know how busy you yourselves are. Maybe you can come and watch the match for a while before you are taken on tour of the establishment".

We did as we were bidden. We viewed the match for a while and saw the future maker of Nepal running up and down the field shoulder to shoulder with his fellow students in a spirit of sincere camaraderie. Then we took the house tour of the world-famous institute from one corner to another. We heard lots of things and asked lots of questions; I lovingly fondled those chairs and tables. And as I did so a long series of historical vignettes flashed past my mind's eye—the chairs hallowed by their association with Sir Walter Raleigh, Lord Nelson, Sir Winston Churchill. . . .'

Chips Channon, you don't know what you've started.

The opposite page carried a large and none-too-flattering photograph of His Majesty flanked by two advertisements; in one of them Nepal Wigs Industries Ltd. humbly offered him a long and happy life, in the other The National Insurance Corporation extended similar felicitations while announcing in the next line 'Starting Life Insurance Business Soon.'

The final effusion was printed in the form of a poem:

> Sweet, simple, noble, sublime, kind,
> Wise Majesty art thou dear,
> Thou rulest all, guard'st with calmness, wit,

Home, subjects lovest with care.

Thou carest no thorns nor fatigue, aches,
Gay walk'st on plain and hill,
Thou toil'st, wipe all's pang and pain
Brisk movest with joy and zeal.

Thou hast keen conscience, foresight clear
And merits, wisdom best;
In pol'tic's knowledge hast thou vast
To tackle, talk and test.

Now, birthday shining twenty-eight thine,
All illumine, joy all round,
With bells of God's blessing, rel'gious rites,
Laud thee all with sound.

'Do you know,' said John when I showed it to him, 'I think I might be able to improve on that.'

Today is the birthday of the King.
The streets are full of people
In coloured clothes,
Tourists with exposure meters aimed
And children everywhere.
The newspapers are full
Of the word 'Auspicious'.
Guns boom loudly and dully
And troops march up and down the roads
And police hold people back
From the middle of the streets,
Where nothing happens hour upon hour.
Since it is a day of celebration
Some of the shops are closed
And the American library
And the British Council.
It is a day of celebration.
Teenagers come out in their best dark glasses
To survey the palely festive sky, but
Whoever is coming does not come

In spite of rumour and anticipation.
People hang from the housetops
Watching other people watching them
And a loudspeaker grates enthusiastically—
Whatever it is saying
Is undoubtedly auspicious.
A large body of men follows, bearing
Yoked pots, strings of goldfish
(The sacred and immortal carp?),
Bamboos, fruit and cabbages;
Then pumpkins, onions, tomatoes and all
Manner of edible and well-grown things.
Scouts arrive—raggedly, then the guides
With efforts at a martial rhythm.
Finally a man comes with a glass box
Containing pink cakes. He rings a little bell—
I am told he is not part of the procession
And trade seems bad today—but it is
A day of celebration, of course.
The pavements empty, and the crowd stands
In the middle of the street—still well policed.
There are no more presents this birthday
And tomorrow, life will move on again
In its dark, weekday clothes
Inauspiciously,
Implacably.

In the evening a power failure drew an appropriate veil over the day's events.

The next edition of the *Rising Nepal* bore some less auspicious news: the Bonington expedition had abandoned its attack on Everest's south-west face, defeated by simultaneous extremes of cold, wind and snow. All those thousands of miles in the Land-Rover suddenly paled into insignificance as we addressed ourselves to the prospect ahead of us.

'That should make it a fair test for us,' Pam remarked, poring again over her maps and counting out her until-now secret hoard of Swiss chocolate.

'For some of us,' corrected Malcolm, who had already voiced the suggestion that to have made it as far as the hashish dens of Kathmandu might be sufficient claim to fame.

In the offices of Mountain Travels Ltd. we were introduced to the two most important components of our support party, Jangbu the chief Sherpa and Pasang the head cook. They made an interesting contrast: the former freshfaced, serious, soberly dressed and with a fair command of English; the latter wizened, jovial, attired in a lumberjack's coat of bright check and a pale blue peaked cap inscribed 'Pinehurst Golf and Country Club, North Carolina' but with a vocabulary restricted to 'yes', 'no' and 'more'.

'Isn't Jangbu a bit young for the job, Fabian?' Bruce queried. (His age was given as twenty-two.)

'Considering that the average life expectancy in this country is only thirty-five, he has to be.'

'In that case I hope to God Pasang manages to push his luck for another five weeks.'

He spoke for all of us.

They accompanied us into the town to help with the shopping. The purchase of the necessary tinned rations had been completed in Delhi, but it remained to lay in supplies of other such necessities as tea, sugar, flour and cooking fat; Jangbu promised that rice, eggs, potatoes and fruit would be freely obtainable en route. He left most of the talking to Pasang, who seemed on very good terms with the shopkeepers—so good in fact that they had our requirements already weighed and wrapped; even more significantly, their prices were not open to the usual negotiation. When we protested, Jangbu assured us with no great conviction that we wouldn't get them cheaper anywhere else, although he must have known that none of us were in a position to put such a claim to the test. Even John's phrase book got him no further than the Gurkhali for 'you must not hold your rifle upside down and rest on it because you will get earth in the barrel'.

As a result we were obliged to cut down on the amounts of our other purchases, which were to read like an exercise in non-alignment: torches made in England, batteries from China, hurricane lamps from Japan, matches from Russia, candles from Pakistan, tent-repair kits from India.

'What about some ropes, Jangbu?' I suggested.

'Ropes is not necessary to Base Camp.'

'Are you sure?'

'Yes. Is necessary only when the weather is very bad.'

'But the weather *is* very bad.'

'Now, yes; soon it will be better.'

'I hope you're right.'

As an afterthought he added: 'If it is not, we can hire at Namche Bazar.'

We left him and Pasang to arrange a means of getting everything back to the hotel and split up on our own individual missions. For me the most important item was something to wear in the evenings as a relief from the climbing boots that I had bought in London: although I had worn them all through the mud of Turkey and had subsequently applied numerous coats of dubbin to them, they still showed no signs of making any concession to the (admittedly idiosyncratic) shape of my feet. The single shoe shop that I could find in turn could only produce a pair of gym shoes two sizes too small. I took them. My other trophies included a dozen bars of Cadbury's Indian-manufactured chocolate, a flask of KAT 29 'Whisky' whose alchoholic content was undisclosed (for excellent reasons, as I later discovered) and a trekking map which carried a rider to the effect that 'in Nepal all paths and bridges are liable to disappear or change at no notice due to monsoons, Acts of God, etc'.

Fabian called a pre-trek briefing. A bus would take us the first fifty odd miles to Lamosangu on the recently built road to the Tibetan border, but after that we would be moving strictly under our own power. The five weeks would be more or less equally divided between the outward and inward journeys; if anyone thought that the return would be quicker, they'd soon find out why it wasn't. The round trip came to something like three-hundred miles, although it was more meaningful to think in terms of height rather than length. Jangbu should be right about the weather. It was usually more more settled in December; there shouldn't be any snow below twelve thousand feet, and above that height it should be frozen hard enough to walk on without too much difficulty—and to sleep on, because we would of course be camping all the way apart from a night in the Thyangboche Monastery guesthouse. The main problem was going to be the effect of altitude, although by then we were all going to be so superbly fit that we wouldn't have much to worry about, would we? Oh yes, there was one other thing—a nasty little complaint called 'mountain sickness', a form of pneumonia which could strike anyone, however fit they were, and kill them within two or three days; the only remedy was to get down as quickly as possible to the airstrip at Lukla, a day's journey below Namche, and fly back to Kathmandu.

An unworthy thought occurred to me. 'Do you have to have mountain sickness before they'll fly you out?'

'What does that mean?'

'Just that I might not feel like walking all the way back.'

'You really have caught the Hillary spirit, haven't you?'

'Once I've seen Everest, it might come as a bit of an anti-climax, that's all.'

' I can't think of a bigger anti-climax myself than kicking round here for a fortnight.'

It was, I had to admit, strictly a choice of the lesser evil.

Thirteen porters had been engaged, Fabian continued, which was rather less than he would have liked, but it was all that our budget could run to: their wage rates had risen twenty per cent in the last year (from ten to twelve rupees a day). We were going to have to cut down pretty drastically on our personal baggage, therefore—to half a kitbag each, in fact; anything over and above that we would have to carry ourselves.

Having been condemned to share one with John, I made the mistake of allowing him first use of it. He filled three-quarters of it and showed no signs of stopping at that.

'I'm going to be allowed a look in am I?'

'Yes, of course. There's only my air-bed to come now.'

' *Your* air-bed?'

'Didn't I tell you? I met this Venezuelan poet who was selling all his stuff off cheap. I'm having dinner with him tonight; you'd better come along and meet him. Francisco's his name; he's quite an authority on Neruda and—'

'Did you buy anything else off him?'

'Only a couple of pounds of green tea,'

'Does that mean you're taking the teapot?'

'I'd like to, of course, but I'm not sure I can find anywhere for it—'

'You don't say.'

'—where it won't get broken: according to Heather, we're only taking a much smaller medicine box.'

'Where's the horn going?'

'In my haversack. I'm just wondering whether I ought to take my tape-recorder.'

'For some yeti noises?'

'Well, I don't know about that, but at least I ought to be able to pick up some Tibetan folk music with it, with luck. I know: if I put the tape-recorder in the haversack then I could wrap the teapot up in my track-suit and get it in the kitbag. . . .'

I decided to cut my losses: there was just time to dash back to the shops before they shut and buy one of the several British Army large packs which I had noticed earlier in the day. I got there to find that they had all mysteriously disappeared from view, and when I did finally run one down beneath a counter its price had jumped from sixteen to twenty-four rupees. The man wouldn't take a paisa less for it; as I forked out, I couldn't help suspecting that Pasang had cornered the market against me. Soon, however, I conceded that it was probably worth even that inflated figure; only my air-bed remained unaccommodated, which I attached to its outside with string.

I went along later to meet John's fellow bard. What he hadn't told me was that their only common language was Spanish, and at the end of the evening I was little more familiar with the works of Neruda. A compatriot of Francisco's, a painter, had come with him to Kathmandu hoping for a year's work, so John relayed to me, but after three months he had failed to complete a single painting, so had packed up and left.

That much at least I could understand.

12   AN UPHILL START

A thunderous hammering on our bedroom door at 5.30 the next morning told us that we were back to our former routine.

The bus was due an hour later, but in fact did not appear until just before seven. It tried to turn in the narrow entrance of the hotel, dislodged a gatepost, vanished into the mist and was not seen again for another half-hour. It was well after eight before everything had been loaded on to the roof and we were finally under way. The old caretaker of the annexe shook his head sceptically as we departed—as well he might.

The porters seated themselves modestly at the back; we were surprised to see three women among them. Their leader was Tsering, a young Tibetan who spoke near-perfect English and played the flute with a facility which put John to shame (without, however, silencing him). After the respective recitals, the others set up a dirge-like chant which was to accompany us all the way to our destination.

We bumped out of Kathmandu over outlying potholes and across the uncompleted extension to the airport's single runway. Long lines of men were already at work on its construction, gouging earth from a quarry with their bare hands and transporting it to the site in wicker baskets. The new road took us more smoothly between fields still green with the winter crop of wheat, past the old capital of Bhadgaon perched precariously on a narrow acropolis and up into a minor range of hills, From the pass at its top we got our first close-up of the Eastern Himalayas, a white strip running the whole length of the horizon; they still looked forbiddingly remote.

'What's the big one in the middle, Jangbu?' I asked.

'This is Gauri Sanka.'

'And how high is that?'

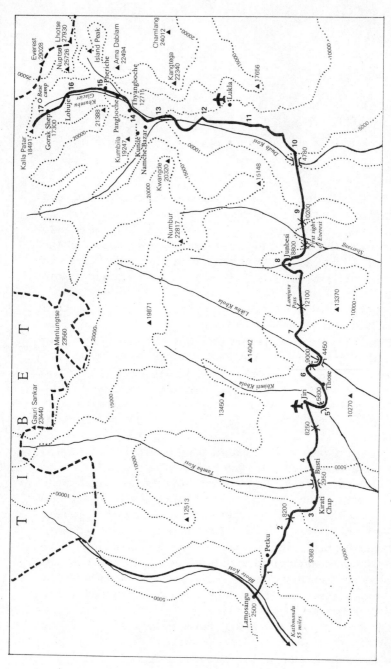

Route of trek from Lamosangu to Everest Base Camp. Numbers 1–17 indicate where the party spent each night.

'Only twenty-three and a half thousand feet.'

Only twenty-three and a half thousand feet: it would make a good lead at my next cocktail party.

When the driver had returned from a lengthy tea-break, we descended to the River Bhote Kosi and followed its course towards Tibet. The sides of the valley grew steadily steeper until at Lamosangu they seemed to rise almost vertically above us. The village, no more than twin rows of roadside shacks, was less impressive, and far from being the bustling terminus that some had expected. The inhabitants looked on dispassionately as we unloaded.

We crossed to the other side of the river by a wobbly suspension bridge.

'Where now, Jangbu? Along the river?'

'No, up here.' He pointed straight up in the air.

'But I thought you said we wouldn't need ropes.'

'No ropes is necessary.' he repeated; his English evidently did not run to such rudimentary humour.

'I don't know how else you think I'm going to get up that.'

'If you look, you will see a path.'

I looked. The whole slope was already in shadow, although it was not yet noon. Gradually I made out a trickle of dust running down from the first ridge back and forth through the tiers of paddy terraces.

At that moment four men emerged at its foot carrying a stretcher; on it was laid one very dead corpse.

Only Pasang appeared unmoved by the significance of the omen.

'Lunch,' he announced.

A meal of powdered soup, spam fritters and Sterotabbed lemonade did little to restore our enthusiasm; still less did the hot sunshine. It took the sight of all our stores and equipment disappearing up the hillside on the backs of the porters to stir us to action.

A 'Last Man' rota was arranged by alphabetical order; the first turn fell to John, although Fabian was heard to express some doubt on the wisdom of including him at all. I was told to hang back with him just to make sure that he didn't interpret his function too literally—rather to my relief, as I was not at all sure how my boots would react to such a test. I was also issued with a whistle with which to supplement his horn in case of distress. Fabian waited only long enough to satisfy himself that we were on the move before striding out ahead.

The paddy terraces soon petered out as the angle of the incline became too much for the Nepali's considerable talent for irrigation. The trail deteriorated correspondingly from beaten earth to bare rock, and at several points progress was only possible on all fours; at others we were in danger of being swept down again by descending parties of porters in their haste to catch the last bus from Lamosangu (even on the best going the manner in which they carried their loads—on a strap suspended from the fore-head—made it difficult for them to see more than a few feet in front of them). Very rarely was it wide enough for us to walk abreast, although this did not deter John from turning round every few yards to discuss Neruda.

'Forcing my brackish semblance through a wilderness.'

'What?'

'It's a line from *The Heights of Machu Picchu*. You know it, don't you?'

'No.'

'Oh. It's his epic on the city of the Incas, but the description fits this place pretty well, don't you think so?'

'Yes.'

'I think next year I might go out to South America and have a look for myself. You wouldn't like to come too, would you?'

'Hm.'

'I'll need somebody who can keep up my pace. I wonder why we haven't caught up with any of the others yet.'

'I wonder why.'

When at last we emerged on the ridge, we saw them—moving ant-like along a traverse to another above it.

At the next corner we were relieved to come upon our three women porters taking a breather. 'Good morning,' they greeted us mockingly as we slumped to the ground beside them and immediately tottered off again (their baskets seemed no lighter or smaller than those of the men). We listened to their shrill sing-song fading into the still air.

Suddenly the ensuing silence was broken by a curious sound, suggesting possibly a cow in labour. We went forward to investigate and found ourselves looking down on a cluster of houses set around a yard. Under the verandah of the largest of them was gathered quite a sizable crowd, all dressed in the Buddhist equivalent of their Sunday best; opposite them were ranged a line of musicians equipped with horns of such prodigious length that they were obliged to rest the ends on the floor. With enormous effort they raised them again and just had time to issue a single, mournful note before gravity reasserted itself. John decided that a reply in kind was called for and blew a blast on his instrument which rolled across to the other side of the valley and back again. The effect on his audience was dramatic: when they had recovered from their astonishment they poured out from the verandah and stood chattering and gesticulating excitedly at us.

'That seems to have livened them up a bit; shall I do another one to really get them going?'

'I'm not sure that I would if I were you.'

Stones began to rise in our direction. They fell only just short.

'You may be right.'

He held up his knapsack to indicate that he was repacking the offending instrument. Gradually the hubbub abated and the crowd returned to the verandah. When everything was again as it had been, two men entered the yard carrying a pole on their right shoulders; something was evidently suspended from it, but we could only guess at what it might be, for it was concealed beneath a brilliant red cloth. They stopped at the entrance to the house; some women then ran out and placed some flowers on the cloth. John had just dismissed my idea of an animal sacrifice as being out of keeping with the principles of the Buddhist faith when another, younger man stepped forward and removed it, revealing a girl lying in a hammock. He helped her to her feet and led her into the house on his arm followed by the rest of the company and a final lowing from the horn-blowers.

We turned to leave, and saw the familiar form of Fabian bearing rapidly down on us. Even from a distance it was obvious that he was somewhat out of humour.

John, perhaps unwisely, sought to forestall him. 'Bad luck, Fabian: you've missed it.'

'Missed what?'

'The local wedding; they've just gone inside for the reception.'

'Look, I haven't just run back a couple of miles to watch a bloody wedding.'

'Have you lost something, then?'

'You, that's all.'

'What made you think that?'

'The sound of your flaming trumpet bouncing all round the mountainside.'

'My horn, you mean?'

'That was actually what I was referring to.'

'I don't see where it comes into it, I'm afraid.'

'For God's sake, did we or did we not agree that that would be the signal that you were lost?'

'Yes, but I didn't bring it just for that; I can do other things on it, you know.'

'I see: I'm supposed to be able to tell the difference, am I?'

'Perhaps you ought to play to the whistle next time,' I suggested.

Fabian was not amused, and said so. He was going to go back at his own pace and God help us if we didn't keep up with him: John could blow on his horn all night but nobody was going to come and look for us.

He set off at a speed which, had we been going down or even on the flat instead of up a one-in-three slope, could with certainty have been described as breakneck. It couldn't possibly last, I kept telling myself; he was only working off some temporary steam on us. But he wasn't: even when we again caught up with the women, he refused to relax. They weren't carrying anything vital—only food, he informed us, so it didn't matter if they didn't make it before dark, but he was going to make very sure that we arrived in time to do our share of putting up the tents. It was now four o'clock; that gave us another hour and a half of daylight.

On and on, up and up we scrambled, stumbled and not infrequently fell. My camera and binoculars banged into my midriff; the sweat poured off my forehead into my eyes; my boots began only too clearly to bear out my earlier doubts about them; the straps on my pack bit deeper and deeper into my shoulders, while the attachment of my air-bed proved so insecure that the only way of keeping it intact was to clasp my hands together behind my back. A constant stream of groans and curses from the rear indicated that John was suffering likewise; certainly he no longer had any breath for Neruda.

The trail levelled out briefly in a small hamlet where a circle of children sat round an old man reciting what sounded like the Nepali equivalent of multiplication tables. As Fabian paused at a house opposite to negotiate for some tangerines, John got out his tape-recorder. In setting it up he made the mistake of playing back some of his last recording, which was that of the Afghan riflemen. The effect was to bring the lesson to a rapid and disorderly close as the children fought each other to get a look at this item of magic. Even when he repacked it and moved on again curiosity was still not satisfied; they followed him tugging and prodding at his knapsack until, goaded into abandoning his ethic of non-violence, he turned and lashed out at them with his flute. A little further on he was able to make some atonement to a group of itinerant monks, exchanging elaborate 'namastes' (the accepted greeting made by bowing with the palms of the hands joined over the mouth) with each of them in turn.

At long last we reached the top of the ridge; I was inclined to think that it was only the tangerines that had got us there. Yet another one loomed in front of us, but some distance short of it a plume of smoke could be seen rising through the trees. This, Fabian assured us, marked our goal, and he was right. According to the map we had climbed almost four thousand feet in the space of the afternoon.

The addition of Richard to the party called for the use of the spare tent, so that John, Bruce and I now had one to ourselves. As soon as we had got it up I crawled into it to make an inspection of my feet, which felt as if they were on the point of bursting into flame. I eased them out of the boots as gently as I could and peeled off the socks which were now stained an ominous red. Both heels had been completely stripped of skin.

Heather and her medicine box could offer little consolation: the best she could do was patch them up with surgical dressings, but that of course would only be a temporary measure; even with the protection of a bandage they would never stay on, given the amount of walking that we had to do every day. The vital thing was to keep them clean until I got back to Kathmandu. (Heather's experience in Skye had taught her all about what became of people who walked around mountains with septic feet.) That was five weeks and God knows how many miles away; how on earth was I going to survive that long? Once before something similar had happened to me, when after a day of platoon attacks on the snow-covered Yorkshire moors of mid-January I had left my sodden boots to dry out overnight on the barrack-room stove. This it had done rather too effectively as I found the next morning when, after a few paces only, the soles had parted from the uppers. For the rest of the day the officer in charge, attributing my sluggishness to a 'lack of enthusiasm and initiative', had followed me into every final assault with a lighted thunder-flash. Not even I was prepared to suspect Fabian of resorting to such an expedient.

In the foulest language I cursed the shop-assistant who had persuaded me to buy these instruments of torture. He had first produced an Italian-made pair lined with fur and superbly comfortable.

'Excuse me asking, sir, but where might you be going?'

'To the Himalayas.'

'Indeed? Then forgive me for saying so, but I am just wondering whether these are quite the right ones for you. I mean, the Italians are, well, shall we say a little decadent, aren't they? Not the sort of people you'd expect to meet on the top of Mount Everest, ha, ha. I have this other pair from Austria which I think you might find more suitable for your purpose; they are also that little bit cheaper, being old stock. Just let me slip them on for you. . . .'

Now I understood why he had been so keen to get them off his shelves.

I then made an even more shattering discovery: my watch was no longer on my wrist. The last time I remembered looking at it was when we stopped for the tangerines; the chafing of my pack against the strap must have eventually worn through it, and being behind my back I wouldn't have seen it drop off. I had to go back for it, I at once decided: besides having a gold case, it had been given to me by my grandfather who came from a long line of clock and watchmakers, and was something of a family heirloom. My mother's last words to me before I had left England had been to be sure to take my spare watch, but in the rush of getting off I hadn't been able to lay my hands on it. I blenched at the thought of her reactions if I returned without it.

It was quite out of the question that I should put my boots on again, and Heather absolutely forbade me to go in bare feet; I would have to make what I could of my undersized gymshoes. By slitting the heels with a razorblade I managed quite a fast shuffle, even if I did have to stop and readjust them every few yards.

I reached the hamlet just before it was quite dark and returned by torchlight. There was no sign of my watch.

I asked Jangbu to enquire of the women if they had seen it, throwing in a reward of a hundred rupees at the same time.

'No, they have not seen it,' he reported.

'What do you think my chances are of getting it back?'

'Yes, you will get it back.'

'How?'

'Someone will find it and bring it to you.'

'What makes you so sure?'

'Nepali people are good people; good, honest people.'

By now I was growing somewhat distrustful of his permanent mien of bland assurance, and I put the same question to Fabian.

'Not a hope,' was his reply, 'especially if it's gold and made in Switzerland: it's the nearest thing they've got to a status symbol here.'

'Well, I suppose there might be a chance if one of the monks picked it up.'

'Don't kid yourself: they're the biggest shysters of the lot.'

The accusation went unchallenged, for John was in the tent reviving himself with a spell of yoga.

As the rest of us sat round the fire avidly watching Pasang and Nyima, his ape-like assistant, prepare the meal, Tsering described China's murderous rape of his country. His family had owned a small farm on the outskirts of Lhasa; they had been forced to billet a company of soldiers on it, all their belongings had been requisitioned, their implements commandeered, their animals slaughtered. When soon afterwards his father had been taken away to a concentration camp they had decided to split up and flee to India. He himself, being only ten at the time, was put under the charge of an elder brother who, however, had been shot and killed within a week. After that he had moved only at night, often going for days at a time without food. Six months later he had crossed the mountains into Sikkim and at Darjeeling had been miraculously reunited with the others.

For someone reared in the comfortable complacency of the West it was a sobering story, and helped to put my own tribulations into better perspective.

For three more excruciating days I hobbled on in my boots, losing still more skin and using up all the dressings that Heather was prepared to allow me. I asked Jangbu where I could expect to buy some more and was informed that there was a chemist's shop at the village of Those. On arriving there I walked up and down the short, cobbled street several times without finding more than a few cakes of Lifebuoy soap in a corner of the single teahouse.

'Where's the chemist then, Jangbu?'

'This is it here,' he said without the least change of expression.

'Well, I can't see any surgical dressings.'

He shrugged his shoulders. 'At Namche you can buy them.'

'I daresay, but what am I going to do in the meantime?'

'At Namche also you can buy boots.'

I made the only decision open to me: I could not possibly go on any further as I was, therefore I would have to resort again to my gymshoes and hope that my feet would heal by the time we got above the snowline. It meant running the risk of turning an ankle over, but I had noticed that none of the porters wore anything more substantial. After an hour spent sewing strips of canvas over the heels with the aid of the tent repair kit, they were ready for service.

The relief was immediate and total; a local anaethetic could hardly have been more effective. I was soon spared even the chore of carrying the boots, for that evening I came across a spare kitbag in one of the baskets. Scarcely believing my luck, I sneaked it into the tent and having transferred them into it together with my air-bed and sleeping-bag, invited John to do likewise. We put it out with the others in the morning and watched in trepidation as the porters made up their loads, but the addition went undetected (until by Fabian several days later, and by then even he was prepared to let it pass as a *fait accompli*).

For the first time I felt free to appreciate my surroundings, and to marvel at how much had been made of such unpromising terrain. Only the very steepest slopes were still uncultivated; on all sides the terraces rose row upon row above us as if in some giant amphitheatre, some no more than a few yards wide. It was evidently the slack period between the summer and winter harvests and there was little activity to be seen, but it was not difficult to imagine the amount of work that had been put into them. Nor had it gone unrewarded: the houses, sturdily built on two floors and neatly thatched and whitewashed, suggested an air of comfortable self-sufficiency, if not actual prosperity. This possibly explained why they were dotted about the hillside rather on the pattern of

Highland crofts instead of being grouped together into communities (only Those had so far aspired to the title of village); or perhaps it was merely that the Nepalis shared the Scots' taste for independence. All the children (and every house seemed to have its quota) looked remarkably healthy considering the total absence of medical facilities. We watched one small boy having a tooth extracted with a pair of pliers; he appeared to think nothing of the experience, and as soon as it was out he ran off in triumph to show it to his fellows.

The flora was mostly over for the year. John claimed to have found a wild orchid in bloom, but before he could produce it for identification by the naturalists in the party he had lost it. Poinsettas—not the spindly specimens in pots so favoured as Christmas presents for those to whom one can't think of anything else to give, but huge clumps twenty feet high and often twice that in girth—did their best to make up for the lack of colour with great splashes of extravagant scarlet.

Of the fruit, bananas and tangerines were just coming into season, which was fortunate for we were already heartily bored of our staple diet of packet soup, tinned meat, rice and potatoes. The trees seemed to grow quite haphazardly and it was hard to tell whether anybody had any claim of ownership on them, although the shifty looking men who hawked their produce up and down the trail were suspiciously quick to move on as soon as they had made a sale.

The teahouses, strategically sited on every pass and river-crossing, were the only sources of refreshment. Unlike their counterparts further west, the *chaie khanas*, these were run by women, usually a formidable figure who presided over the fire suckling a baby with one hand and stirring the tea already mixed with milk and sugar in a saucepan with the other, while the older children saw to the washing up and the supply of firewood. Their scale of charges was often hard to follow and to make matters more complicated still, they refused to change any note larger than one rupee until it occurred to them that they were not going to get paid at all unless they did. This reluctance was explained by a commendable distrust of paper money and by the fact that the bank was kept either in the recesses of their underwear or in the tin trunk they were sitting on.

They frequently fell foul of Bruce who, like all true Yorkshiremen, kept a keen eye out against any sharp practice.

'You pay two rupees.'

'How much?'

'Two teas, fifty paisa—'

'Wait a minute, you said it was fifteen paisa a glass.'

'Small tea fifteen paisa, large tea twenty-five paisa.'

'Bloody hell, you don't call that a large tea, do you?'

'One biscuit, one rupee.'

'One rupee, for those? They were only seventy-five at the last place.'

'Three bananas, fifty paisa.'

'You said two cost thirty, so that only makes forty-five for three. That's all your getting, anway. Here's one seventy-five.'

'You pay two rupees.'

'Look two teas, thirty paisa, right?'

'Large teas, fifty paisa.'

'*Small* teas . . . .'

By this stage there would be no one left to report how the argument was resolved.

Soon these luxuries, such as they were, began to pall too, so that when Jangbu spoke of the possibility of a visit to an experimental farm set up by the Swiss at Jiri, my first reaction was to ask him what we could expect to find to eat there. The reply of buffalo steaks seemed excessively optimistic even from him, but at least it held the promise of something more than tea and biscuits.

We were taken on a lengthy conducted tour. It surprised only by its lack of surprises: in the cowshed we found a herd of Friesians; in the pigsty, Saddlebacks; in the sheep-pen, Blackfaces; in the chicken run, Plymouth Rocks. Something of our sense of *déjà-vu* must have been transmitted to our guide, an earnest young graduate of Delhi University, for he then launched into a description of the exotic wild life that lurked in the woods only just above where we were standing; it included tigers, leopards, bears, hyenas, wolves, boars. However, the only evidence of this that he could produce was a slightly oversized cat stretched out on the rail of a balcony. Closer inspection proved it to be long dead.

Was there any thing else that we'd like to see? Well, there was this canteen where our Sherpa had told us we could get a decent meal. Ah yes, so one could normally but he was very sorry, the cook happened to be away today. Of course if we would like some, he could probably arrange some tea and biscuits. . . .

Jangbu gave no sign of contrition when confronted with the news. 'At Namche you will be able to get buff steaks.'

'Is that a promise?'

'Yes, with chips also.'

'Namche must be quite a place.'

'Yes, Namche is a big place, the most important place for Sherpas.'

'I'll make a deal with you, then: if you find me a new pair of boots, I'll buy you a buff steak and chips. All right?'

'All right.'

The day's most bitter disappointment was still to come, however. As a result of our diversion the evening meal was awaited with more than usual impatience, but when it was served one mouthful was enough to warn us that something had gone very, very wrong.

For Hugh, who had found it increasingly impossible to satisfy his youthful appetite on the fare to date and had already exhausted his pocket money in the teahouses, it was the last straw.

'What the bloody hell do you mean by serving up this shit?' He raged at the unfortunate Pam.

'I don't know why you should blame me: I only told them to make up a stew with some of the tinned meat I got in Delhi.'

'And what was that?'

'I'm not sure; have a look at the label on the tin if you really want to know.'

He did. It bore two words: Bombay Duck.

13   HARD CHEESE

On the seventh day we crossed the Lamjura Pass, just over twelve thousand feet high.

It had been anything but a gradual ascent: from our second night's camp at 8,200 feet, we plunged down more than five thousand to the Tamba Kosi gorge overlooked on either side by the settlements of Kiratichap and Busti (soon amended to Karate Chop and Booby Trap respectively by JC, who had a genius for such things—it was thanks to him that in Istanbul the district of Tepebasi had become the less forgettable 'Teddybasher'), up five thousand again to the next pass, down another two and a half, up three and a half, down four and up no less than seven to the Lamjura and our first contact with snow, lying frozen on its northern slope.

'The blurb didn't lead us to expect anything like this,' I grumbled to Fabian.

'Well, if it had, no one would have come, would they?'

I had no answer to that.

Nor was I the only casualty. Malcolm, unable to persuade anybody to stay behind with him in Kathmandu and now anxious to prove that his motives in trying to do so were quite removed from any distaste for physical exertion, had set off at a startling pace, but he soon faltered and fell back until even I was overtaking him. He complained firstly of cramp, then of strains and finally of blisters, but Heather confided to me that the dressings she conceded him were more to comfort his morale than his feet. He fashioned himself a staff from a length of bamboo and this, together with his straggling beard, made him as much a figure of woe as an Old Testament prophet consigned to the wilderness.

Fabian, unmoved as ever by the frailties of others, strode on in the lead even though he was carrying his own kitbag to save porterage; Richard's long, wiry legs did their best to keep up with him, but the rest were content to rely on the more lackadaisical Jangbu for directions.

Of the girls, it was June who surprised most with her stamina; 'it's doing wonders for my figure,' she explained—as indeed it was, Malcolm maliciously observed. Heather showed the dogged cheerfulness associated with district nurses, and in the midday heat her cheeks came near to matching the scarlet of her ever-present tam-o-shanter. For some time Pam succeeded in maintaining the guise of the dedicated mountaineer, but gradually the rising chorus of complaints about the food seemed to get her down; it was not until we got back to Kathmandu that she was discovered to have contracted hepatitis.

John's progress was, as ever, unpredictable; at some times he would suddenly bound ahead in pursuit of a multi-coloured bird or butterfly, at others he would stand motionless, lost to the world in contemplation of remoter horizons:

> The hills speak
> With a slow, solemn voice.
> Once they danced
> In the early light,
> Sang and trembled
> In the beginning of the world;
> But now the first men
> Sleep beneath the sun
> And those who walked alone
> And sang the rhythmic songs
> Have gone away.
> Now the hills are alone
> And speak with the slow voices
> Of old men, who tell
> Of another time,
> In the still air,
> In the earth,
> Where no one listens.

The Lamjura marked the beginning of true Sherpa country. Prayer flags were strung across the passes, ripped to tatters by the wind; the trail was divided every so often by *manis*, long rows of stone tablets inscribed with Buddhist lore; one or two of the villages boasted *chorterns*, shrines decorated on each side with the all-seeing eyes and benign features of the god.

Jangbu's home lay two hours off the main trail beyond Junbesi, the next village. In return for our help with his English homework he asked John, Bruce and I back to stay the night with him. John had already set his heart on a visit to a monastery higher up the valley, but Bruce and I readily accepted the invitation—half in curiosity, but half also in the hope of a substantial meal.

It was already dark when we left Junbesi. Jangbu led the way with a hurricane lamp, but he went at such a pace that we were frequently out of range of its light, leaving us to make the best we could of the numerous tree stumps and other obstacles. 'It is not far', he kept replying to our repeated question, although after an hour he did condescend to pause for a few minutes while we ate the last of the day's biscuits. We met no one, and the few houses that we passed were in total darkness; only the barking of dogs told us that they were there at all.

We emerged at last from the forest and in the wan moonlight saw some more houses ranged on the hill opposite. Jangbu's was one of these. Like most Sherpa houses it was on two floors, the lower one a stable; we could hear some cows shuffling and snuffling about in the straw. Upstairs the house was divided by a partition into sleeping and eating quarters. The only light came from the central fire where Jangbu's mother, small and wizened, sat stirring a steaming cauldron of *rakshi*, a spirit distilled from rice; she was making it for the market where she had a stall, he explained. We were introduced in turn to her, his sister who looked about fourteen and his much younger brother. None of them greeted him with the least show of emotion; it seemed to be an accepted fact of Sherpa life that the menfolk disappeared for months at a time. They were little more excited either by the presents that he had brought them, although these were admittedly of a functional nature: a pair of socks for his mother, a pullover for his sister, a tin of boot polish for his brother, a razor for his father who now emerged from the sleeping quarters, rubbing his eyes.

Room was made for us round the fire and the *rakshi* circulated. Only the brother, who attended the Edmund Hillary school at Junbesi, spoke any English and he only a few words, so that the conversation was a bit stilted, adding to the anticipation with which we watched supper being prepared: omelettes, spinach and a great pile of potatoes which Jangbu peeled, not very effectively, with a sickle. The sister kept very much to background, scurrying about on various errands, while the brother astonished us by taking the pots from the fire with his bare hands and holding them while his mother served. We were not disappointed in either the quality or quantity of the meal.

When it had been cleared away another great copper cauldron was brought up, this time of *chang*, a potent but not very palatable brew made from maize. It seemed that this was what the old man had been waiting for: until now he had hardly spoken, but he now began burbling away in a low voice. It was evidently a story, the gist of which Jangbu translated for us as follows:

'Many years ago there lived a number of yeti above Namche Bazar. Their habits caused a lot of trouble to the people who lived in the village. In the daytime the yeti used to sit on the hill watching the men cutting the grass to make hay and planting potatoes. Then in the evening they used to come down when the men had gone home and tried to copy what they had done, but they were very clumsy and succeeded in destroying most of the crops. The men worked harder and harder to grow more, but the yeti always undid what they had done.

One day the villagers collected to discuss what could be done to stop this, and they made the following plan: they carved a number of wooden statues and when they had finished them they got together bowls of *chang* and *rakshi* and put them into the hands of the statues. Then they attacked the statues with sharp knives, cut them up and threw them into the river. That night the yeti came down as usual and copying what they had seen the men do they attacked each other with the knives that the men had left behind. In this way they were all killed except for one female who had just had a baby and so had been unable to come down with the others. When she saw that all her companions were dead, she fled higher into the mountains and to this day the yeti have never come down again.'

When he had finished, the two children tiptoed away to bed looking as if they expected a sleepless night.

After several more rounds of *chang* we followed them, rather less light-footedly.

John appeared somewhat out of humour when we rejoined him

in the morning. We did not have to wait long for an explanation. It had been a long, hard climb up to the monastery and he had got there rather later than he had intended—only to be told that it was just about to shut for the day. But he had come to stay the night, he had protested. They were sorry, but there was no room except for visiting monks. Well, at least he could have a quick look round. No, he couldn't. Why not? Because the Lama was about to begin his meditations. He could join him, then: he was a Buddhist himself. No, that was quite impossible. So they were going to let him come all that way for nothing? He was welcome to sign the visitors' book: the charge for that would be one rupee.

It had almost been enough to make a Christian of him; he hoped to God (*sic*) that Thyangboche wasn't going to be like that. Then to cap everything, he had got lost in the jungle on the way back. He had blown his horn, but no one had come to look for him; instead they'd simply replied with their pathetic tin whistles which of course he hadn't heard until he'd been wandering round in the dark for a couple of hours, by which time they'd eaten all the supper. . . .

We thought it kinder not to describe our own meal to him for the time being.

After an hour of gradual ascent we emerged above the tree-line and rounded the side of the hill. A whole new range of mountains now opened up ahead of us; on its extreme left one peak stood a little behind the others, a plume of snow billowing from its crest.

Everest.

It was a magical moment; all the discomforts and privations of the past two months seemed suddenly worthwhile.

I said as much to John.

'It looks the same as any other bit of rock to me,' he muttered and stumped on.

Pam asked to borrow my binoculars and glued her eyes to them until the lenses began to steam up. 'That must be the south-west face,' she concluded. 'That's the rock-band just below the South Summit; Chris always said it was going to be the toughest part.'

'Chris?'

'Bonington. Apparently it's so hard you can hardly get a piton into it. See that other peak at the right end of the range—do you reckon it's Makalu I or II?'

Nobody ventured an opinion, and we left her once more spread-eagled over her maps.

Descending into the next valley, we came upon a procession of Tibetans dancing and singing up the trail towards us and led by a man waving, of all things, a black umbrella; how he had come to obtain this symbol of City Man was a matter beyond conjecture.

John's spirits rapidly revived as he hurried to unpack his tape-recorder.

The accompanying flutes, drums, horns and cymbals certainly gave off an impressive volume of sound, although to the ears of the uninitiated there was no very clear theme to it; moreover, some of the party were obviously drunk. They had good reason to celebrate, Tsering informed us, for in the previous week they had managed to escape across the border, now heavily guarded; they brought reports also of continuing guerrilla warfare in the remoter areas against the invader. Presently they paused in their exertions to offer us a rather dull selection of rings, necklaces, medallions and other items of religious significance, all at prices which even John found himself able to resist. The one real collector's piece, the umbrella, was not for sale.

Later, John played back the tape for the benefit of the porters. They watched mystified as it unwound in total silence. After trying twice more with the same result, he was forced to admit that in his excitement he must have forgotten to switch on the microphone.

The next morning we crossed the Dudh Kosi, the main river of the Everest region. According to the map we were now down again to under five thousand feet, a height we had exceeded on our first day out; the knowledge put something of a dampener on the enthusiasm generated by that first sight of our goal.

We turned to follow it northwards between the towering pillars of Numbur (22,817 feet) and Chamlang (24,012 feet), but we were soon compelled to abandon it for higher ground when it vanished between the vertical walls of a ravine; in the next three days we had occasional glimpses of it thousands of feet below. We saw little also of the sun, which was only able to penetrate into the valley for a couple of hours either side of noon even when the sky was cloudless, which it seldom was now. Crop cultivation was no longer a practical proposition, and the terracing at last gave way to juniper forests and yak pastures. Our first encounter with these delightful creatures was on a narrow bend; they seemed quite as suspicious of us as we were of them, and their drover, a boy of no more than ten, was reduced to tears in his efforts to coax them past us.

At the next house John suddenly disappeared through the front door on some unexplained mission and re-emerged a few minutes later the triumphant possessor of a large cheese. It proved a timely purchase. That evening Pasang subjected us to the Sherpa delicacy of Dildo, a peculiarly unappetising compound of flour and maize mixed with water to make a stiff paste; the only thing to be said in its favour was that it very effectively stopped up our intestines for several days afterwards.

It could do nothing for our bladders, however, and the combination of cold and altitude drove each of us from the tent three or four times a night. The fact that we never seemed able to synchronise these excursions led to bitter recriminations in the morning; the first to succumb inevitably woke the other two as he groped his way out; they would then lie thinking that they ought to be joining him but postponing the awful moment for as long as they dared, by which time the first would be just on the point of getting back to sleep again, and so the whole grim cycle would be repeated.

As we settled down for our last night before Namche tempers were as short as the stubble of our nascent beards.

I had not been asleep long when I was roused by a violent tug on my leg.

'Michael.' It had to be John. 'Are you awake?'

'I am now, yes.'

'Sorry, but this is serious.'

'Couldn't you hold it?'

'No, it's not that. There's an animal in the tent.'

'Another cat, I suppose.'

'Another one?'

'Unless the same one's followed you all the way from Persia.'

'Look, this isn't funny. I'm worried about the cheese.'

'I'm not surprised, the amount you've eaten. No wonder you're dreaming of cats.'

'It's not a dream, I tell you. Can't you hear it?'

'No.'

All the same, I pulled the cord of my sleeping bag even tighter over my head.

'You might have a look with your torch.'
'Not bloody likely.'
'Give it to me then.'
'It's under the top of my bed.'
'I can't reach it there.'
'That's tough.'
'A fine friend you are, I must say.'
'Yes.'
The conversation lapsed into muttered obscenities.
At reveille John was, uniquely, the first to stir from the tent.
He returned moments later clutching his cheese. Even in the semi-darkness his fury was unmistakable.
'That animal you said I was dreaming about, you know what it did, don't you?'
'I can't imagine.'
'It only got hold of this and dragged it outside, that's all.'
'Well, it still seems to have left most of it for you.'
'And a fat lot of good it is.'
'It looks all right to me.'
'Just you try and eat it, then.'
I tried.
It was frozen solid.

> Damn this place where no one but the bold
> Dare bare their bums to the opprobrious cold.
> Where home is both a message and a tune
> But cannot be too silver or too soon.
>
> If I get cold, I want a warming fire
> Without the need to build a funeral pyre;
> If I get wet, I want to dry my socks
> Without the need to lay them out on rocks.
>
> I don't want fingers falling in the snow,
> I want a rum and Christmas-pudding glow;
> I don't want feet encased in blocks of ice,
> I want the feel of curry, extra hot with rice.
>
> I don't want to be frozen, famed and dead—
> All ambitions of this kind have fled,

I want a hot-potato death in style—
To disappear fast as a miser's smile.

I want a place where people close the door,
Where people sit on chairs and not the floor—
Some place indeed much like the Rosslyn Arms,
Far from blizzards, snow and mountain charms.

So please, Lord, save me from these mighty mountains
And take me where the Watney's runs in fountains—
I want *beer*, not *tsampa, chang* or even *rakshi,*
Plus that famous final fumble in a taxi.

14 MINOR TRIUMPH, NEAR TRAGEDY

After another mile or so the trail descended briefly to rejoin the river.

Several rows of tents were pitched on the near bank, enough to quarter an average infantry regiment. Their occupants were found to be American, not Chinese as some feared. There were twelve of them, we learnt, as there were of us; the difference lay in the comparative strength of our support parties—theirs numbered seventy as against our seventeen. They were clad in voluminous parkas and double-quilted trousers which made them look like Michelin men and they sat in deckchairs at collapsible tables eating a breakfast of eggs, sausages, tomatoes, sweetcorn, cookies and cranberry jelly helped down with fresh coffee.

A short, gnomish man in rimless spectacles introduced himself: 'Granville's the name, Granville Devitt. You just down from the airstrip, are you?'

'No, we've walked here.'

'From Kathmandu?'

'More or less.'

'Is that right? Did you hear that, Al? These guys have made it all the way here on foot.'

The crew-cut giant sitting beside him lowered the cookie in his gloved hand and looked me up and down, dwelling at some length on my gymshoes.

'Jesus,' he said finally.

Well, he had to hand it to us, Granville guessed; they themselves had just had a week at the Everest View, the hotel recently opened above Namche by the Japanese, two hundred and fifty dollars all-in including the two-way air-fare. The room service hadn't been quite what they were used to back home and they hadn't got any iced water in the bar, but for that sort of money what could you expect? Besides, they'd seen some of the cutest villages and the view of the mountains had been out of this world, just out of this world. In his, Granville's, considered opinion, that was the right place for mountains—the other side of a double-glazed window. And as for climbing, well, we could keep that too: from now on he was going to stick to the top of the Empire State for his fresh air. They were fixed to fly out that afternoon; I wasn't going to tell him that I was crazy enough to walk all the way back again as well, was I?

During this conversation I had seen a small, single-engined plane climb lazily into the sky and head down the valley, and in that moment had come to a decision.

'No.'

After promising to look him up the very next time I passed through Long Island, I took my leave.

A little further on we came across an even more bizarre figure, a one-legged Swiss accompanied by a single Sherpa. Our map marked Namche as having a hospital and in some apprehension John asked him how long ago he had lost his leg. During the war, came the reply, but it had not stopped him from climbing most of the big peaks in the Alps and only the symptoms of mountain sickness had prevented him from reaching Base Camp. The weather was more settled now higher up and if he could get that far then we were going to find it twice as easy, weren't we?

We laughed mirthlessly.

Another ravine closed in again on the river, forcing us once more upwards and above the tree-line. We caught a second glimpse of Everest, now only twenty miles away; the snow still billowed off its crest towards the east.

'Looks a bit draughty up there,' Bruce said.

Nearer at hand, the peaks of Kwangde (20,320 feet), Kumbila (19,247 feet) and Kangtega (22,340 feet) rose like the sides of a bowl around us, and twenty miles took on a different meaning from the distance between Staines and Hyde Park Corner.

Presently four or five rows of ramshackle, stone-roofed houses came into view, set in the shape of a horseshoe between two spurs of the mountainside. Surely this couldn't be Namche Bazar, the great wen of chemists, hospitals, bootshops, steak-houses and climbing-equipment stores?

It was.

We selected the only level open space available for our camp site. The natives had their own uses for it, as we very soon found out; John, Bruce and I adjourned in haste to lay claim to a space for the night in the Sherpa 'Hotel'. This comprised a single, rectangular room arranged round a central fire, its low ceiling blackened by a thick layer of soot. Two window seats and a table provided the sleeping accommodation for the early comers (which fortunately we were); later arrivals had to make do on the floor. An old man shuffled forward out of the gloom to greet us; his back was bent so low that his *namastes* seemed directed at a point halfway up our shins. His wife, similarly aged but more mobile, offered us glasses of tea from a steaming cauldron. The charge for our board (one meal) and lodging, she informed us, would be six rupees or fifty American cents if we had them (no quotation in sterling was given); it seemed eminently reasonable.

Having established ourselves, we set out on a tour of the village. An exhaustive search yielded a post office and two shops. The former, situated above a stable and approached by a flight of rickety steps, was open but empty.

A boy who had been sunning himself in a doorway nearby got to his feet and walked over to us.

'He has gone,' he observed.

'Where?' Bruce, who wanted a stamp, asked him.

'He is my brother.'

'Yes, but where is he?'

'The postman is my brother.'

'So you said before, but where can I find him?'

'He has gone.'

We gave up.

In one of the shops we were informed that the postman would not be back now until ten in the morning.

The Fair Price and the Cooperative Store stood opposite each other. 'Stalls' would be a more accurate description of them: apart from local produce—potatoes, eggs, rice and still more potatoes—they offered only a few items of exotica sold off as surplus by expeditions returning from Everest—Mars Bars (the genuine articles all the way from Slough) for five rupees each, jars of peanut butter for twelve, tins of pineapple for twenty. There was no sign of any surgical dressings.

I confronted Jangbu with the fact.

'At the hospital you will get them,' he asserted with undiminished confidence.

'Here?'

'No, it is at Kunde, the next village. Up there.' He indicated somewhere just short of the top of Kumbila.

I decided that perhaps my feet were healing well enough to be able to do without them.

'And the boots? I didn't see any in the shops.'

'My friends will have some. I will ask them.'

After an hour or so he returned with three pairs. Needless to say, they were all several sizes too small for me.

He still had a chance to redeem himself. 'What about those buff steaks, Jangbu? Don't tell me they're up at Kunde as well.'

'No, they are here.' There was just a hint of evasiveness in his voice.

'Where?'

'At the teahouse.'

'Can you take us there?'

'Yes.'

'Now?'

'If you wish.'

'Yes, we do. We've waited a long time for these.'

He led us along a narrow path between two terraces and up another wooden staircase into a dark room.

'These are they.'

We peered about us and presently made out shrivelled strips of smoked meat hanging from the ceiling.

'These?'

'Yes.'

Just for good measure, the surly proprietress informed us that they were 'off'.

A generous helping of rice and vegetables back at the hotel provided some compensation. We were joined there by Don and Harry, two young Canadians on their way down again to Lukla. Harry had been up as far as Kalla Patar, a minor ridge overlooking Base Camp, but Don had suffered too badly from the altitude to accompany him; its effects still showed in his face, its pallor highlighted in the glow of the fire. They hadn't actually booked a flight, but from what they'd heard they could expect to get off in a day or two; we wouldn't be interested in buying the dried fruit they had left over, would we?

They could hardly have found three better people to ask.

When the meal was over, Jangbu, Pasang and all the porters filed in and settled round a brazier of their own (to which they transferred a considerable portion of our fire) for a session of *chang* and an interminable song which could have passed for the Nepali version of 'Old King Cole'. Whatever it was, its monotony very quickly sent me into a profound slumber, notwithstanding the appearance of a mouse beside the pillow of my air-bed.

I was roused some hours later by a sound of rustling paper from the corner where we had stowed our baggage. My immediate thought was that the mouse must have got at the remnants of John's cheese and I discharged a volley of apricot stones in its direction. The noise persisted, however, until at last I got up to investigate, and found that it was caused by the cellophane which covered the window flapping in the wind.

We rose at the strange hour of eight o'clock to a still stranger breakfast of porridge, fried eggs and potatoes, tea and biscuits. Others besides Bruce had business at the post office; none of their letters ever reached their destination, and it was only later that we learnt that they would not have been put on a plane at Lukla as we had expected, but taken all the way to Kathmandu by runner. In the meantime I climbed up to the police station which was set on the ridge overlooking the village to report the loss of my watch. After making a tortuous transcription of my statement into Nepali script, the sergeant told me that nothing could be done for the present as the radio transmitter was out of order. Outside, a squad of Gurkhas were performing prodigies of drill on a square which measured no more than ten yards in length; at any moment I expected to see them march obediently over the edge of the precipice in the best military tradition.

The morning's stint—a gentle traverse of Kumbila's lower slopes in warm sunshine—was by common consent the most pleasant of the entire trek. Not the least agreeable feature was the fact that the day's destination could be seen almost from the start instead of being concealed from us by a succession of ridges, each one leading us to believe that it was the last. Thyangboche lay perched on the crest of the next spur, its pagoda-style roof clearly visible above the trees; beyond, the end of the valley reared upwards into the climactic triangle of Nuptse (25,726 feet), Lhotse (27,930 feet) and Everest itself (29,028 feet). Another, unexpected treat awaited us: rounding a corner, we came across a covey of gorgeously coloured pheasants. Their heads were blue-green, their necks pure gold, their bodies royal blue and their tails orange, each part equally brilliant; they strutted about uttering shrieks of indignation that such humdrum creatures as ourselves should have dared to invade their kingdom.

We descended to the river for lunch; it was the last chance we would have for a week of doing any washing. I could just bear to bathe my injured feet in its icy waters; although they were mending well, I still dreaded the moment when I would have to submit them again to the boots.

A climb of some two thousand feet lay in front of us. John strode on ahead with the fervour of a true convert, but when we met up with him again at the top it was evident that this had cooled somewhat. With good reason: instead of a thriving community of fellow-believers, he had found the whole place deserted except for one monk with a limp, who had informed him that the Lama (a little inferior only to the Dalai himself in the hierarchy of Tibetan Buddhism) and the rest of his colleagues had gone to pay their respects to another monastery. Poor John! I tried to console him with the thought that at least he would be able to meditate in peace.

Having relieved us of two rupees each, the monk took us on a tour of the monastery. It was not as old as the style and intricacy of its decoration suggested, having replaced the original building which had been destroyed in 1933 by an earthquake (the present Lama's predecessor had not surprisingly perished with it, being 85 at the time). The meditation hall was a long, dark room, sparsely furnished with benches, cassocks, twin tambours suspended from the ceiling and a pair of enormous, telescopic horns which I remembered from a television documentary on the Sherpas as needing two men each to operate, one to blow, the other to carry the far end; it was also intensely cold.

For another two rupees we were allowed the run of the 'Guest House', a wooden shack equipped only with a small, ancient stove, although how such an item had got there in the first place was anybody's guess. What to feed it with was no less of a problem, for the only sources of firewood were a few pine trees and giant, gnarled bushes of rhododendron; some earlier guests had had recourse to the floorboards. By dusk, however, we had amassed quite a pile of branches, not all of them combustible, and it was found necessary to start a secondary fire below the grate.

By the morning the cold was again victorious: I reached into my sponge-bag for my flannel and found it frozen like a cricket ball. The sun was still behind the mountains when we abandoned John to his solitude; he made a desolate figure, and we parted with expressions of hope that Bruce's photograph would not be our last sight of him.

The tenacious rhododendron yielded finally to scrub and heather just below the village of Pangboche. At a height of nearly fourteen thousand feet, this represented the last point of permanent habitation; above it lay only the temporary settlements used by the yak herdsmen in the summer and a couple of teahouses. Its *gompa* contained a skull which was boasted to be that of a yeti, although Pasang let us know what he thought of the claim by getting down on all fours and grunting like a pig. Jangbu looked faintly shocked.

The skyline to our right was dominated now by the soaring mass of Ama Dablam. Although a mere twenty-two and a half thousand feet, it was perhaps the most dramatic of all the mountains that we were to see; its apex of glistening ice jutted vertically into the sky, earning it the rather insulting title of the Matterhorn of the Himalayas. Even John might have been impressed. To our front Everest gradually withdrew again behind the great wall of Nuptse as we got nearer, like Salomé behind her seventh veil. The going was surprisingly undemanding—the snow was confined to stretches of dead ground and north-facing slopes hidden from the sun—and we reached the head of the valley by mid-afternoon. Here it split into two subsidiary valleys which led in turn to the Khumbu and Imja glaciers. The latter was divided by a ridge running down from Lhotse and ending in a buttress which Bruce identified on Pam's map as Island Peak. From where we were it didn't seem to present too difficult a climb, and it had the added attraction of being just over twenty thousand feet, a height which we had no chance of attaining anywhere else. We agreed to have a crack at it on the way down from the Khumbu, the weather and Fabian permitting.

We stopped for the night at Pheriche, one of the summer settlements. We began an inspection of the yak stables in the hope that they might make a better defence against the cold than our tents, but one look into their dank, evil-smelling interiors had me beating a rapid retreat towards the teahouse to apply for accommodation there. It was already well filled with a party of Japanese and their Sherpas, but a space was found for me on a bench. The porters evidently arrived at the same conclusion for they appeared en masse a few minutes later and arranged to sleep on the floor. The rest of the group followed shortly afterwards and advanced with shaking hands on the fire, having also finally abandoned the stables; they left me in no doubt of the hardships involved in putting up tents in such a temperature. The obliging young proprietor told us that he had been up as high as twenty-six thousand feet with the Bonington expedition, a fact which did something to explain the extraordinary range of provisions on his shelves, running even to a tin labelled 'Fortnum & Mason Lobster Soup'. I assumed it to be an Indian imitation, but when he got it down for me I was soon convinced of its authenticity by the directions: 'Dilute with a little milk, and white wine if desired. The addition of some cream or butter with a dash of brandy. . . .' My KAT 29 would do for that; I told him to put it aside for me. His equally amiable wife nursed an infant at her breast; in June's professional opinion the lack of any proper hygiene should have killed it at birth, but it seemed very much alive to me. The Japanese were earnestly sorting out their equipment; their Sherpas told me that they too were hoping to get to Island Peak, but due to the recent snow they were not optimistic of their chances, even with ropes and crampons. To Bruce and me it began to look like just another nice idea.

The porters greeted me somewhat sourly in the morning; it seemed that I had trodden on most of them in the course of my several sorties during the night.

A lengthy discussion took place over breakfast as to where the next stop should be. Fabian was all for pressing on to the top hut at Gorakshep (17,300 feet) which would then give use a full day's climbing in the Base Camp area, but Jangbu was doubtful that the porters could be persuaded to go beyond the teahouse at Lobuje (16,175 feet). By way of compromise it was eventually agreed to lunch at Lobuje before making a final decision depending on how much of the day remained.

The sun was now up and for an hour we made pleasant progress along the floor of the valley, encouraging me to think that I could postpone my boots for one more day. This brought us up against the Khumbu glacier's terminal moraine, a feature every bit as imposing as it sounded: I had the feeling of being confronted by an inverted, thousand-feet-high steam pudding with boulders for currants. As we clambered up it the lack of oxygen soon made itself felt until at the top we had only enough breath left to plead with Fabian to stop for lunch. He would have none of it, however, and when the cooks plodded stoically past we had no option but to follow.

We were now on the glacier itself; under the snow I was surprised to find not ice but loose earth and stones. My gymshoes made hard work of it, and it was a relief to cross over to firmer ground on the far side. In spite of the freshness of the snow there was already quite a well-defined track through it, albeit only a foot wide so that any stray step was liable to send one plunging off it.

Lobuje was reached none too soon at 12.30, a time which seemed likely to bear out Jangbu's prediction, and when after another hour the porters still had not arrived Fabian conceded the point. Set on a bare shelf so close to the wall of the glacier that it was in shadow by two o'clock, consisting of two dilapidated huts and permeated by a pungent stench of human excrement, it would be difficult to imagine a more uninviting spot. On the other side Nuptse reared up almost sheer for another ten thousand feet, its face streaked with great cataracts of ice which periodically broke off and crashed down to the glacier with an ominous rumble.

We climbed up the ridge immediately above in pursuit of another half-hour's sunshine, then descended again to the chill business of putting up the tents. Our puny tent-pegs made no impression whatever on the frozen ground, and we had to scrabble around for suitably sized stones. This done, we adjourned to the hut denoted as being the teahouse (the other one was quite deserted) by a miserable little fire in one corner. We had not been there long when a man and a boy entered with a load of firewood. As soon as he saw us the man rushed over to a shelf beside the fire and began counting the few packets of biscuits which were stored there. Then he turned and launched into a torrent of what was clearly something other than a speech of welcome.

'He says that you have stolen some biscuits,' Jangbu explained to Fabian.

'We haven't touched his lousy biscuits. You can tell him we didn't even know they were there.'

This reply moved him to even greater excitement.

'He says that he must see who has taken them.'

We all stood up and turned out our pockets.

He was still not satisfied, however. 'He says you have eaten them.'

'And the wrappers too, I suppose.'

'He will look in your tents.'

'Oh no, he won't.'

A prolonged, triangular argument followed. In the course of it the boy must have slipped out unnoticed, for he now reappeared and held out something towards his father which Bruce instantly recognised as his.

'You little bastard' he exploded 'get your horrible, thieving grubbies off my Mars Bar!' Whereupon he lifted him up by the collar and shook him until he released the precious item.

The Rubicon had been crossed, the father's shriek of outrage seemed to indicate.

'He says you must go now,' Jangbu confirmed.

We huddled together in one of the tents wondering who was going to yield first: it surely wasn't every day that brought him twelve customers, but on the other hand we had seen enough of him to suspect that there was no limit to his malevolence. Outside, Nuptse gleamed like a giant nugget of gold quartz in the dying sunshine, while directly overhead a full moon took premature form.

It was not quite dark when we were surprised to see a wild-eyed figure with long, blonde hair approach unsteadily up the track.

'I shouldn't go in there, mate,' Bruce warned as he went past, 'they'll strip you naked,' but he staggered on into the hut.

A few minutes later Pasang announced that supper wouldn't be ready for at least another hour. The collective will crumbled, and Jangbu was sent to negotiate the terms of surrender. He reported them to be that our tents would be searched, that we could only stay as long as we drank his tea (at one rupee a glass) and that under no circumstances would Bruce be allowed in. Bruce retorted that under no circumstances would he ever pay such a price for a glass of tea, let alone to him.

No biscuits were of course found, and we were grudgingly

admitted. The latest arrival was laid out on the floor in considerable distress; between moans we learnt that he was Dutch and had come straight up from Lukla in three days. He asked if there was a doctor or nurse among us. Heather told him bluntly that there was nothing she or anyone else could do for somebody who had done what he had, except to commit him to an asylum. The second condition of the treaty was rigidly enforced: as soon as anyone's glass was empty it was made very plain to them that they had either to buy another one or go. I put my sopping socks and gymshoes up on the hearth to dry, but they were immediately knocked away. I replaced them as soon as his back was turned, only to have them removed once more by the boy. Bruce had chosen a misnomer to describe him: no two were ever more obviously father and son. After four glasses (including one taken out to Bruce) I abandoned the attempt.

It was still only six o'clock when we finished supper, but short of bankrupting ourselves on tea there was nothing else to do except don every bit of clothing we possessed and crawl into our sleeping bags. Even in my tracksuit, trousers, pyjamas and Long Johns it was some hours before I was warm enough to sleep and for Bruce, who was sick several times, the night was still more uncomfortable.

'The sod must have put something in my tea,' he muttered.

Such a possibility was not easily discounted.

The dawn broke cloudless and windless for this day of days, this day that was to bring minor triumph and near tragedy.

After a breakfast of porridge and raisins (we had run out of sugar) we stood round Pasang's fire thawing out our boots which had set rigid overnight. A few wisps of smoke began to rise from the teahouse, but the boy evidently thought that his best chance of some warmth lay with us and he hovered about waiting for a gap in the circle. His presence was too much for Bruce, who drove him off with a few well-directed snow balls. The Mad Dutchman then emerged. Although he looked even ghastlier than he had done the previous evening, he waved aside all Heather's pleas that he should stay where he was for a day and set off. We followed a few minutes later, and it was no surprise to meet him stumbling back again the opposite direction, this time retching horribly and spewing blood. We never saw him again.

Although the track now led over the snow rather than through it,

the sight of my frozen boots persuaded me to persevere once more
with the gymshoes in the hope that the crust would be hard enough
to support me. For a while it worked and I made good speed
skating over the top, but as the sun's strength increased, so the
crust became less reliable; several times I found myself sinking up
to my knees, then having to fish about in the hole for my shoe. The
dazzle of the snow was now almost more than the eye could bear,
even with sunglasses; two of the porters had been foolish enough to
come up without them and they began to flounder about like a
couple of drunks. Later the wall of the glacier became too steep to
traverse, forcing us out on to the glacier itself and over a series of
moraine ridges. Not only were these quite stiff climbs in
themselves, but the track became extremely difficult to follow
between the boulders and, once lost, was only regained after much
trial and error.

We passed a line of ice sails, curious triangles of ice rising twenty
or thirty feet out of the moraine. Ahead of us Changtse (24,720
feet) came into view above the saddle between the sugar-loaf of
Pumori (23,190 feet) and the still-invisible Everest, which marked
the Tibetan border. On our left we could now make out Kalla Patar
(the Nepali for 'Black Rock')—a dark ridge running up towards
Pumori. Gorakshep, a pair of tiny huts, lay tucked under it on the
edge of the glacier. It was just as well, we all agreed, that we hadn't
tried to make it the previous day.

Lunch left us with another four hours of daylight. The majority
opted for Kalla Patar, but Bruce and Richard announced that they
were going on to Base Camp; they were the only two climbers in
the party and they claimed that the place had some mystical
significance for them, even though Fabian pointed out to them that
they would not be able to see Everest from it.

I had seen enough of Kalla Patar to conclude reluctantly that my
boots were no longer to be denied, and in this I was soon justified.
Climbing out of the trough of the glacier, we were confronted first
by a plateau of snow not knee, but waist-deep, then a long scree
leading up the ridge itself. On the latter little crust had formed
between the rocks, and more often than not it was a matter of
wading through the snow from one to another. At a height of
eighteen thousand feet this is not a form of progress to be
recommended.

Fabian, still wearing the tattered jeans and faded brogues in

9 Loading up in Kathmandu

10 On trek

11   Thyangboche monastery

12   Mine host with lobster soup at Pheriche

which he had left London, struck out for the higher, right-hand end and soon far outdistanced the rest of us. I struggled in his wake, prodding at the snow with the handle of the ice-axe that Jangbu had lent me. (Jangbu himself had stayed behind on the pretext of 'guarding the camp'. It was difficult to know who he was expecting to be attacked by—except, of course, the yeti. The only animal I had seen since the yaks was a slightly oversize, tailless hamster which had popped out from under a rock at Lobuje for a quiet nibble at a discarded potato. Perhaps he feared that the species was gathering for an assault on our guy ropes in the manner of the mice who had made such a meal of the Assyrians' bowstrings.) It was not until I was half way up that I turned to find that the others were making for the lower end. Fabian was now nearing the top and having committed myself this far I decided that I might as well go the whole way with him. I called to him to wait for me, but he was already out of earshot and soon, as the incline increased, out of sight as well.

The snow got still deeper. I tried to keep to the rocks as much as possible, even at the expense of a considerable detour. Several of them wobbled rather alarmingly until, pushing my luck too far, I landed on one which promptly set off down the mountainside, tipping me headlong into the snow in the process. As I hauled myself out of it and groped around for my camera, binoculars and ice-axe, some suitably ribald comments floated down from somewhere above. I looked up and saw Fabian sitting on the summit a hundred yards further on.

A few minutes later I collapsed like a burst balloon beside him.

'According to the Royal Geographical Society we are now at eighteen thousand, four hundred and ninety-one feet,' he informed me.

'I can believe it,' I gasped.

'Well now you're here, what do you make of it?'

'It's. . . .' I paused to look around me, but even when I had got my breath back, the words still wouldn't come. The view quite literally defied description. Only now were we able to appreciate the full sweep of the glacier below us; it was as if a pair of gigantic snow-ploughs had scoured its walls, pushing the debris into the middle in great jumbled piles. Beyond, Ama Dablam still dominated the southern horizon, lording it arrogantly over its fellows; to the west the two Changri glaciers plunged down from twin ridges and collided in awesome concurrence; to the north the ridge dropped sheer for a thousand feet, then bounded up again to rejoin Pumori; to the east, revealed at last above the blue-green cascade of the Khumbu icefall pouring out of the Western Cwm, stood Everest, dark, menacing, magnificent.

Overhead, mountain crows cackled their mockery of our insignificance. Presently they lost interest and drifted away, taking with them all thoughts of what I had gone through to get here. Never before had I felt such a deep sense of tranquillity, of remoteness from the turmoil of life, of being alone and at peace with my Creator.

I wondered whether John had been able to achieve a similar state of bliss in his chosen surroundings.

Like all such moments, it was soon over.

'I think we'd better move before it gets into shadow,' Fabian said. 'Can you see the other two anywhere?'

I searched up and down the glacier with my binoculars for Bruce's red anorak, without success.

We went more or less straight down across the snowfield. The crust was already freezing hard again and we were able to slide for long stretches on our backsides. It was too late, however, to save my feet: two hours in the boots had undone all the recovery of the past two weeks. Jangbu greeted us rather casually for one who had been sitting guard all afternoon against potential invaders.

Bruce and Richard had not yet returned, and I hobbled up to the first ridge on the glacier for another look, but there was no sign of them.

Dusk fell, and still they had not appeared. By now I was distinctly worried, remembering how Bruce had suffered the previous night; I could find little of my usual appetite for supper. At seven o'clock it was agreed to send out a search party under Nyima, who had spent two months at Base Camp earlier in the year cooking for an expedition and claimed to know the way up to it blindfold. I felt rather ashamed at not offering to go with them, but the condition of my feet made it out of the question. Instead, I organised a half-hourly rota of whistle blowing. The whistle's echo bounced back and forth between the walls of the glacier, but there was no reply. The cold and solitude reminded me all-too-vividly of my many futile patrols of the Catterick tank park, except that no lives were ever there at stake.

The search party returned just before midnight, empty handed; Nyima thought he had seen their footprints, but that was all. There was nothing more we could do until the morning.

I lay beside Bruce's empty sleeping-bag rehearsing all the things that could have happened to them. They might simply have got lost; one of them might have been injured and the other not have had enough daylight to go back for help, or, more likely, the altitude had finally got the better of Bruce; perhaps they had got too near the ice-fall and had fallen down a crevasse; or perhaps. . . .

The possibilities were endless. Conjecture gave way to morbidity: without proper clothing, equipment or food, would they even survive until the morning in such an extreme temperature? As long as they kept together they ought to be able to, but it was by no means certain. Never before had I passed a night in such discomfort of body and spirit.

After a hasty breakfast the same party set off again for Base Camp, Jangbu went down to Lobuje to see if they were there and if they weren't, to continue to Namche and radio for a helicopter, while the rest of us spread out over the glacier. As we advanced into it another eventuality prompted itself, for the ridges became increasingly treacherous: at the slightest provocation—or even sometimes of their own volition—boulders would break away, setting off a minor avalanche in their wake. If they had tried to cross these in the dark. . . .

I walked down the entire length of one without seeing so much as a footprint. Then as I stood wondering how to get across to the next one, I noticed a distant figure coming up the glacier from the direction of Lobuje. I trained my binoculars on him: it was Jangbu. Fabian ran towards him and returned with arms aloft.

They were safe.

In the teahouse Bruce explained what had happened. It had taken them longer than they had anticipated to reach Base Camp, and in their haste to get back they had missed their tracks, confused an inner ridge for an outer and strayed out into the middle of the glacier before, at dusk, discovering their mistake. Correctly deciding that it was then too dangerous to cross back over the ridges, they had found a small hollow for themselves, built a rudimentary shelter of stones round it and settled down together for the night, keeping themselves awake with songs and a distribution every quarter of an hour from their meagre hoard of chocolate. Daylight had given them no better idea of their whereabouts and they had gone on down the glacier until they had hit the main track, which was where Jangbu had found them—hungry, exhausted and slightly frost-bitten, but very glad to be alive.

After another night at Lobuje I was almost prepared to admit to a sneaking sympathy for its two inhabitants.

The sky the next day was overcast and a biting wind blew up the glacier, giving us still less reason to hang about. Fabian reckoned that we could easily make Thyangboche that evening.

I stopped at Pheriche just long enough to collect my lobster soup and to learn that the Japanese had failed in their attempt on Island Peak.

15 MEANWHILE, JOHN BACK AT THYANGBOCHE . . .

I followed the others down the slope and said goodbye for the next few days.

At first I was filled with a pleasant sense of peace and freedom; alone at last, I thought. However, this feeling was soon replaced by another, slightly less agreeable, as I returned to survey my accommodation and my stores. Out of the general stores that sufficed for the whole party, I had been given two tins of fish and a couple of packets of biscuits, together with five rupees a day; on this I was supposed to survive until the others returned. Unable to convert myself into a mouse like the giant in Puss-in-Boots (in which case this lavish provender would just about have lasted), I realised that things were not going to be as easy as I had thought.

I was now also the supplier of my own firewood, and I soon turned to this occupation, determined that I should at least be found warm and in possession of all my fingers and ears on the return of the others, albeit in a state of grubby emaciation. I didn't have much luck, for the others seemed to have successfully picked the place clean the previous evening. All the dead pine branches within reach had gone, while the rhododendrons appeared so hardy as to be almost immortal. I returned to the guest house with the meagre fruits of my search and sat considering the empty stove.

Presently there was a tap on the door and the lame monk entered. I examined him at my leisure. Though his methods were primitive, he was undoubtedly a shyster of the first order. He exuded a sort of grovelling ruthlessness with each gesture and painful sentence. It was also clear to me that he slurred and mumbled half-comprehensibly so as to give the impression of a

native witlessness that he thought I would be deceived by, and by
which he hoped to further his inscrutable ends. I marked however
how his eye glittered and knew the seeming for something other
than the reality. I seldom had to explain myself twice to him, except
where money was concerned and in that instance, he was merely
giving himself time to think whether or not he could plead for a
rescission of the contract, jack the price up 50 per cent, or claim
that he had overlooked some overhead or other which would make
his quoted price impossible to maintain.

I enquired of him whether the Sherpa hotel was in operation,
but it was apparently closed until further notice for reasons I did
not fully understand—then or indeed ever.

He then volunteered the information that there was an
establishment vacant that vied in splendour and creature comfort
with the lamasery itself. As I had not seen the interior of the
lamasery, I did not feel obliged to quibble with this statement; and
as for the guest house, I was fast coming to the conclusion that my
only chance of any warmth there was to set fire to the remaining
floor boards, and even that drastic remedy would not have seen me
through more than one night. I went with him across the barren
quadrangle which may one day become the central square of some
monkish metropolis, but which was now the private stamping
ground of a solitary yak, and in through the doorway of what was
to be my new home.

A long dark passage used for storing firewood led into a square
room with a partly boarded floor and wooden-framed windows
covered with sheets of cellophane. I asked about the rent and was
informed that it was one rupee a day. After some consideration, I
agreed to this and moved in. I brought my bundle of firewood
across and seizing his chance, the monk offered me more from his
private supply, at which point the ramifications of the monastic
marketing system became clear to me. One rupee didn't buy much
firewood. One rupee bought one egg; a dish of potatoes cost three
rupees; the monk was the only one around to sell them. He
admitted they were cheaper further down but the extra was
accounted for by the cost of carrying them up to Thyangboche. I
saw people carrying all sorts of odd things in the Himalayas, but
never potatoes. I began to contemplate my future and my five
rupees a day with increased alarm.

Ruefully, I purchased three eggs and some of the potatoes,

which the monk was considerate enough to boil for me, as I had no cooking pot. I ate frugally, keeping the remainder of the potatoes for the evening, when I hoped to have the fire going properly and to bake them in the hot ashes.

At this point the monk's boy appeared. He was apparently a youthful adherent of the monastery (if not of the faith, as I later found out to my cost). The boy seemed lively and bright-eyed, but showed signs of a sharpness that turned towards cunning rather than intelligence. His English was quite good, and he was justifiably proud of it, being a pupil of the Hillary school in Junbesi. Seeing that I had purchased some wood from Mr Big, the boy explained to me that the monk's wood was not very dry or of a very high quality for burning, and that he himself had a secret store of wood that was all that could be desired. He took me to the hiding place which was a large dry shed on the southern side of the hill. I bought a few rupees worth from him and did not think it strange at that time that the monk's wood should be out in the open though covered up, whereas his small charge should have a proper storage place for his own wood.

As soon as the money was in his hand he vanished, leaving me to the silence of my own company.

> Though December is nearly ended,
> The valleys are still full of sun—
> But the monastery is deserted.
> It is said the high lama is away
> Visiting an even higher lama
> On business of some kind. No doubt
> They will compare potato prices,
> Profit margins, markets, et cetera.
> Up here, the matters of the spirit
> Are distant as the mountain peaks
> And somewhat less in demand
> And less well-rooted,
> Than the humble spud.

Instead of making the best use of the timeless atmosphere of the place, the Western devil in me took over, and I began to construct a sun clock, with a tall stick and figures engraved in the snow. The job occupied some portion of the afternoon, together with several

more sightings taken when a stray traveller with a watch passed
through the grounds in pursuit of higher things. Most people I met
later seemed to think that I should have gone higher up myself,
even if not actually scaling mountains, but I said that as I could see
the top of Everest from the doorway of the hut and the only
purpose in going higher was to see the bottom of the celebrated
crag—which is undoubtedly even uglier than the top—I should
stay where I was. The evening came on, and I cursed the fire into
some sort of life and plugged some of the gaps in the window (but
not all, for there was no chimney). Outside, though it was not yet
dark, the moon had risen with a promise of brilliance, and a couple
of hours later, the whole valley was filled with its pure, silver light.
There seemed to be some strange partnership between the sun and
moon, and the light of one seemed to replace the light of the other
without a pause. I remembered walking home on just such a clear
winter night in Sussex and my path on that occasion ran through a
birch wood; the scene here was on a grander scale but could never
produce the thrill of those moonlit woods with their delicate
tracery of shadows and half-seen shapes.

I stoked up the fire and proceeded to settle in for the night on
the raised plank that served for a bed, first shaking out the
motheaten yak-skin rug and putting it under the sleeping-bag so
that the cold would have a harder time getting at me from
underneath.

I also barred the door securely.

The next morning I stayed in my sleeping-bag until the sun came
up, which was well after nine o'clock. Shortly afterwards, the monk
reappeared and asked after my welfare with unctuous solicitude. I
rashly ordered another plate of steamed potatoes for my lunch,
and began to wonder what the hell I was going to do with myself
for the next four days; by this time I had given up all hope of
putting myself in a meditative mood and so profiting by my
isolation. I went across the parade ground to examine my sun clock
and decide to improve it by setting up a table of hour-angles by
which I could check its accuracy at different parts of the day. This
interesting and entirely useless labour successfully took up most of
the morning.

Emerging from my deliciously plutocratic lunch, I was startled to
see a vast American in a gleaming blue parka, sitting on a stone at

the side of the parade ground. I resisted the terrible impulse to rush up to him and start talking nineteen to the dozen, and instead affected to examine the scenery about me for a few moments before smiling in his direction and remarking on the landscape and the weather. This tactic apparently struck the right note, and he realised he was in the presence of a true Britisher and therefore a man to be taken account of. We exchanged courtesies (his name was Dave) and fell to a discussion of objectives; we could go up to Dingboche to see the fabled yeti skull, but I had reliable information that this cost the astronomical sum of ten or even fifteen rupees, and for that you were ushered into the long-dead presence of something that resembled no more than a wizened coconut; or we could go down to the village of Kumjung and visit the Everest View Hotel—probably the highest in the world (at thirteen thousand odd feet). We both agreed on the latter. During this conversation, his girl friend, Louise, arrived and to demonstrate my hospitality I invited them into my quarters for a drink of hot water. They accepted, and, to my great relief, produced some coffee to put in it.

Scenting business, Mr Big soon arrived, nervously brushing down his robe at the thought of the possible avenues of success into which his financial expertise could lead. He showed us some more potatoes and some really small pullet's eggs which he had clearly been saving for the arrival of a group, so that he could sell them en bloc on the very slight chance of refusal. Dave began to haggle, which seemed only reasonable as the price demanded for the eggs was still one rupee each. The monk would have none of it, however, knowing that we must either pay the full price or go hungry; he merely stood there in the doorway with an odd sly smile on his face and refused to budge. In the end we had the doubtful satisfaction of buying less than he wanted, but less than we wanted as well. I added the potatoes left over from my lunch to make up the gap.

Afterwards we sat warming ourselves by the fire before turning in. Dave, a faraway look in his eyes, said little but still radiated a large presence. Louise was a complete antithesis: dark, attractive, vivacious, she made up for his silences by her light, down-to-earth humour. I soon realised I could trust the pair, because whatever doubts I had about Dave's coolness, I could already see that she acted as a firm conscience for him, and was in the process of training him into a considerate attitude not merely in relation to herself. I was shortly to be very thankful for this.

The next day, we left fairly late and had our lunch in a clearing beside the river Dudh Kosi, some of whose waters had been diverted to drive a huge prayer wheel.

The way to Kumjung was misty and uneventful, except for the strange views of clouds hung over the deep valleys. One appeared from our angle like a flat plate of silver, until the sinking sun came round one of the peaks, and at the touch of the light, the cloud suddenly lost its glow and became grey and sinister, while the thin beam of sun remorselessly cut it in two like a torch.

We stopped to rest about half-way along the last stretch to the village. I reached for the cigarettes in my anorak, which I had attached to my haversack, and found to my horror that it was no longer there.

I arranged to meet the others later in the village, and pounded back down the trail. I met one or two people and questioned them, but of course they knew nothing. I did not worry so much about the loss of the anorak, which I had brought because it was old and on its last legs, but in the pockets were two treasured books—one of Hafez and Saadi and the other Snodgrass. Not only this—for the books were at least replaceable at a later date—but also my irreplaceable woolly Peruvian-Indian hat and, perhaps worst of all, my last twenty rupees.

I made my way dolefully back to Kumjung, which did not look at first sight the sort of place to raise my spirits, in spite of being the biggest Sherpa settlement in the whole region. I met up with the others, and after a leisurely inspection of the village we decided on a Sherpa 'hotel' for the night. I explained my misfortune to Dave, who after some prompting from Louise, offered to pay for my board and lodging; I agreed to pay him back in Kathmandu and surrendered my camera (whose shutter was jammed) as collateral. We found there two Australians, each with his own Sherpa guide. While our supper was being prepared, we watched bemused as the two Sherpas ate the contents of a large bronze vessel, which must have contained about five or six pounds of potatoes. If they ate in such a princely fashion in Thyangboche, I calculated that one meal would have cost them two days wages. However, the Australians were paying, which no doubt stimulated their appetites. Our meal, which consisted of the usual rice and spiced greens, and the accommodation came to about four rupees apiece; both were good value. Afterwards, several glasses of tea were drunk round the fire before settling down on the various window seats and spare patches of floor, which the proprietor had considerately strewn with yak-skins for our comfort. Despite my sudden penury, I soon slid off to sleep, only too grateful to be out of the clutches of the robed Rachman of Thyangboche.

In the morning we all made our way upwards to a narrow defile which rose precipitously into the mist to the invisible and eminent eyrie of the Everest View Hotel. As we approached it, I raised my great buffalo horn and gave a blast or two to signify our arrival. This precipitated a vast and ferocious dog down the front steps of the hotel, barking furiously and apparently hungry to get to grips with foreign bodies. To our considerable relief, the dog's approach was halted with a twang and a strangled snarl as it reached the end of its tether. We edged around it slowly enough to count its well-kept fangs and entered.

There was not a soul in sight.

The place was no warmer inside, in fact considerably less so, since outside the sun was shining strongly. We clumped about for a few minutes inspecting the building, which was complete but for a few additions which were under construction. Soon a yellow parka appeared at the desk, surmounted by a smiling Japanese face.

'Yes please, what may I do for you?'

'I was wondering if I could book a flight back to Kathmandu here.'

'Of course, that is very easy. Every day we send runner to Lukla.'

'How much is the fare?'

'Two hundred rupees—eight pounds sterling for Englishmen.'

'Unfortunately I haven't got that much on me at the moment.'

'But you can pay when you are back in Kathmandu.'

'Really?'

'Yes, of course, just you sign piece of paper, please, that is all that is necessary now.'

I also booked a seat for Michael and made out the appropriate IOU to the Royal Nepalese Air Corporation. The thought that in four days time I would be released from my incarceration in the mountains made even the prospect of returning to Thyangboche seem almost bearable.

We ordered some tea and sat drinking it with the Sherpas, who were in a merry mood and seemed much to enjoy their opulent surroundings. The manager explained that the hotel was empty for considerable periods of time and was mostly used by parties on all-in, a-thousand-dollars-a-head Asian tours. The hotel airstrip was under construction nearby and, he hoped, was going to make all the difference, Lukla being a couple of days away on foot. On one side of the hotel there was a huge window with a breathtaking view out over the mountains across the valley, and nearby a large round, raised fireplace with a hood over it so that the customers wouldn't have to move from the fire to look out of the window. This was no doubt where Granville had set himself up for the week.

We paid up—we were charged half the price on the menu—and made our way down past the plateau where the airstrip was being completed and the control-tower was a recognisable skeleton. Nothing very much seemed to be going on, so we headed for Namche, that sybaritic metropolis, that caravanserai through which all trade and pleasure passes, that store house of Mars Bars, for which I have such a terrible and consuming weakness. Unfortunately I had no current account in Namche, and I judged Dave unlikely to advance me any more towards what would seem to him so frivolous an investment.

After a short tour of the place (and any tour of Namche is necessarily short) we split up to make our own arrangements for the night. I went into the Sherpa 'hotel' where I was again impressed with a sense of sufficiency and good management. There was almost a full house and in honour of the occasion the proprietress had prepared a variety of Sherpa dishes: a spicy noodle soup, omelettes, potato dal, a tasty type of cannelloni with real meat inside called Mumu—not to mention the dreaded Dildo. These were followed by milk, tea or cocoa, or salty buttered Sherpa tea if one's fancy happened to veer that way. In short, if I had any business to be in the Himalayas at all (and of that I was increasingly doubtful), I decided that this was the place for me.

The other customers included two Danish girls. Although they both spoke English and I spoke Danish, I did not get very far in my conversation with them. This might have been due to the shortage of women and its attendant nuisance value to them, or perhaps

13 Mission completed: Fabian and Everest

14 Lukla airstrip

15 Phantom railway, Baluchistan

they thought I understood more of their conversation than was actually the case; at any rate, they kept out of my way. Besides them, there were several assorted foreigners including a lone young Englishman dressed in a rather ridiculous pair of plus-fours and who spoke in an unpleasant tone of affected arrogance. He delighted in telling me how successful he had been in obtaining a tear-gas pistol in Germany on the way through. He then asked me how we had got on with the Turks, to which I replied that we had found them more hospitable and generous than anyone on the entire trip. This seemed rather to amuse him.

'All I can say is you must have been damn lucky, or else there were more of you than they could handle,' he said. 'A gang of them tried to mug two of us in eastern Turkey, and it's lucky that I happened to have the gas pistol on me—that sorted the sheep from the goats, I can tell you.'

For various reasons, this story neither fitted the honest Turks I knew nor any Turkish robbers I had ever heard about. My suspicions about the character of this specious young man began to grow apace. He then embarked on another good-luck story, about how fortunate he had been to buy some canisters of CS gas in Persia, which had come in very handy in putting to flight another band of brigands in Pakistan.

His purpose in visiting the mountains—or indeed the East at all—was obscure; it seemed that he had not come out of interest, but rather to demonstrate something to himself or perhaps the unfortunate world at large.

I made a point of laying my sleeping bag in the opposite corner to his.

After another excellent breakfast, I addressed myself to the disagreeable necessity of returning to Thyangboche. A chill wind whistling up the valley behind me made sure that I kept on the move.

There was no sign of my anorak.

I found the monastery still deserted. However, it was a considerable compensation to find the 'hotel' now open, thus sparing me further negotiations with Mr Big and his rascally acolyte. Sitting on a bench the other side of the fire was a darkish man of medium build whose nationality I could not place, though I thought at first that he might be Asiatic. As I went up to greet him I realised that this was an incorrect impression, but there was something about him that was not European. I said a few words to him but he smiled at me and spread his hands apologetically saying 'No English'. I asked in my bad French: 'Vous êtes venu de la France, peût-etre?'

'Uruguay', he chuckled at my surprise. I immediately switched over to Spanish, and he breathed a sigh of relief, his French being no better than mine. We were soon conversing fluently. I told him of my rather forlorn hopes to immerse myself in alien cultures and broaden my experience so that I would have plenty of fresh material when I returned hom.

'And has it worked?' he enquired with a smile.

'No,' I confessed 'but I had a suspicion that it wouldn't in the first place.'

'Yes', he said 'when you create something, it is from the image that you carry round inside you all your life; it does not go in through your eyes, but comes out through your hands and lips according to the skills you have learned.'

After this, it was no surprise to discover that he was a sculptor. We talked late into the night over innumerable cups of tea.

The next morning he set off for Everest and I was once more alone.

Outside it had clouded over and I spent all day huddled close to the fire, writing.

My rest is burning wood,
My going ash;
Cold drives me on.
I hear wings in the still air
Invisible and vast;
Spirit of stone.

I lie between mountains
Themselves enfolded by the moon
Whose winter radiance
Turns all to marble.

I linger like a grey feather
Uncertain of the wind;
The prayer flags are thin and torn,

Moving at an unseen touch
In search of lost gods.

Through the open door
Snow, and still prayer wheels;
The logs burn down,
The water simmers softly
And the hours
Flow away like smoke.

Late in the afternoon I heard voices and going to investigate I saw the familiar column straggling up the path through the rhododendrons.

They seemed quite as surprised to find me still whole in mind and body as I was them.

16   LAST LEG OF THE TREBLE

Three days later John and I took our leave of the others at the turning for Lukla. In another three days it would be Christmas; hopes of mutual comfort and joy were exchanged. We tried not to sound smug; they talked bravely of the tinned pudding that they were going to celebrate it with half way up the Lamjura Pass. Bruce embarrassed us further by presenting us each with a small offering carefully wrapped in lavatory paper.

We still faced a climb of over a thousand feet, made more arduous by the fact that we were now our own porters. Without the aid of headbands we made heavy weather of it, stopping every hundred yards to shift our kitbags from one shoulder to the other. At one of these pauses John contrived to drop his; the top burst open and out poured the flutes, the telescope, the air-bed, the tape-recorder, *The Heights of Machu Picchu*. . . .

I helped him retrieve them from the bushes, keeping an anxious ear cocked for the sound of an engine.

I need not have worried.

The airstrip was no more than a rough clearing perhaps half a mile long and tilted at an angle of some ten degrees to the valley. A two-engined freighter plane with a broken wing stood propped up in a corner; it had clearly been there for some time and looked as if it was going to remain there still longer. The small knot of spectators, porters and would-be passengers who stood around its perimeter had an air of phlegmatic resignation about them, rather like that of a Test Match crowd at Lord's staying on after a heavy thunderstorm to await the umpire's inspection of the pitch in four hours time.

I was surprised to find the two Canadians we had met at Namche among them. Don still looked distinctly out of sorts.

'I thought you were hoping to fly out about a week ago,' I said.

'That's right, we were,' Harry replied, 'until that bloody crowd of Yank bums fouled it all up. Their charter plane packed up, so they moved in on the regular service. It took the whole week to get them and all that gear out.'

'Bloody bums,' Don agreed.

'So you're going today?'

'I wouldn't count on it: the Boss says it depends on the weather.'

'It looks all right to me.'

'So it did yesterday and nothing turned up.'

'We're booked on today's, but it doesn't look as if that means very much.'

'You can say that again,' said Don.

The office of the Royal Nepalese Air Corporation was housed in a tent. The Boss, a prosperous-looking young man dressed in a luxurious parka, repeated what he had said to Harry. I asked him about the wreck and he told me cheerfully that it had crashed coming in to help another plane which had also crashed; there was nothing left at all of that one. He also ran the teahouse next door, a rather more substantial affair; at fifty paisa for a small glass, it was clear where he made his money.

We found ourselves a sunny corner out of the wind and settled down for a long wait.

At one o'clock there was a faint stir of anticipation and a woman went so far as to shoo off a yak which had strayed on to the runway; but that was all. An hour later there was another stir and this time a plane did arrive; no one got on board, however, and it immediately took off again—not for Kathmandu, we learnt on enquiry, but for Darjeeling. At four o'clock, just when the Boss declared that it was now too late for any more that day, another appeared over the ridge on the far side of the valley and came into land. It was a single-engined Pilatus, and almost before it came to rest it was besieged from all sides by the waiting Sherpas who seemed to think nothing of the risk of being cut to pieces by the propeller; they tore open the doors, crammed their luggage into the tail and piled in themselves. The Boss looked on helplessly until the pilot roundly informed him that he only had room for five passengers and two hundred pounds of luggage, and that if he didn't take off in five minutes he would lose his licence; he then moved in and started pulling them off again by the first limb that came to hand until he had reduced them to the prescribed number. The co-pilot's seat was granted to Don because of his condition; he was strapped into it looking greener than ever. The doors slammed, the plane swung round and they staggered off into the twilight.

We adjourned with Harry to the teahouse and were joined there by an American surveyor who had been reporting on the airstrip of the Everest View. Much to the consternation of its Japanese owners, he had found it to be seventy degrees out of its proper alignment. However, an auspicious solution was at hand, for tomorrow His Sublime Majesty himself would be arriving to bring his foresight clear to bear on the problem.

We passed the night on the table which served as the Royal Nepalese Air Corporation's desk and woke to the rantings of a Buddhist engaged in his early morning devotionals on the floor.

When I complained, John remarked bitterly: 'You don't honestly expect religious fanatics to think of other people, do you?'

Not even our joint rendering of the *Te Deum* could shut him up.

We were content to breakfast on tea and biscuits, so near did we feel now to the prospect of plenty. When two hours later nothing had happened it began to look as if such confidence was misplaced, and we returned for a second sitting. The Boss assured us that he was expecting a plane any minute now, and even as he spoke, we heard it—at first a distant murmur, then welling into the unmistakable sound of our deliverance.

We rushed out to see for ourselves that it really was so and found not one plane, but two—the Pilatus followed immediately afterwards by a twin-engined, fifteen-seat Otter. For a moment I was afraid that they might be the preserve of the King and his entourage, but they were both empty. We made for the latter, threw ourselves into the nearest available seats and dug in behind our kitbags, determined to ward off all comers—quite unnecessarily as it turned out, because we took off with only five other fellow-passengers.

In a matter of yards we were airborne, seemingly without having climbed at all. A wave of turbulence hit us as we cleared the first ridge, but already I had no mind for anything but the awesome vista opening up on my right. Presently the whole range of the Nepalese Himalayas was visible, from Dhaulagiri in the west to Kangchenjunga three hundred miles further east; in the centre

Everest waved farewell with her snow-plume handkerchief. It was not a sight that I shall quickly forget.

Below us the passes and valleys, the rivers and terraces slipped away, and with them the memories of aching legs and blistered heels, of sweaty socks and frozen flannels, of dim teahouses and fuliginous hotels, of sour porridge and boiled potatoes—not to mention Bombay Duck.

They were, we both agreed, the best £8 we'd ever spent.

The Snow View was only prepared to offer us a double room in the main building at thirty-five rupees each. We declined it, but not before we had availed ourselves of the luxury of its lavatory (not that there was anything especially luxurious about it, but it did make a gratifying change from a rhododendron bush—or worse). The Shanker was still more expensive, the Kathmandu Lodge cheaper but full, the Camp rather too suggestive of its name, the Oriental no more than a row of cupboards.

We found our Valhalla at last at the Panorama; for twenty rupees, a spacious room, sprung mattresses, 'full breakfast' and a bath—three feet long and made of stone, but still a bath. There was one small drawback: the immersion heater provided only enough hot water to fill it once every four hours.

We tossed for first use.

I won.

> Michael hums,
> Whistles,
> Radiates.
> The sound of hot water in torrents
> Drives him to song, like a stag in spring.
> The water gurgles liquid accompaniment,
> A bubbling woodwind obbligato
> To his rapt baritone.
> The voice rises and falls—
> 'People stop and stare, they don't bother me . . . .'
> Swish goes his hand and the water responds with heat.
> The voice rises again robustly, fervently.
> 'There is nowhere else on earth that I would rather
>   beee. . . .'
> He quavers, momentarily.

O desolate month in the mountains
Deprived of all this. Nothing but cold water, cold
   air,
Cold ground and plain rice.
The voice rises again to a final roar:
'That overpowering feeling. . . .'
Then silence. Utter silence
But for the plashy dribbling of the water.
This is the supreme moment.
It approaches sublimity.
Swish.
Gurgle.
Ecstasy.

The final bliss was reserved for my battered feet: clean socks and the freedom to expand again inside my Moroccan slippers. When I had said goodbye to them as old friends a month earlier, I had scarcely appreciated the strength of my attachment.

My stomach was soon claiming its share of attention. We had provisionally arranged to meet Harry for lunch at the Hungry Eye, but the Indira was the first restaurant that we came across.

We stopped and looked at each other.

'Might as well go in and have a look,' John suggested, 'just for future reference.'

Once inside, not all the horses of the Apocalypse could have dragged us out again.

'It was only a provisional arrangement, wasn't it?' I said. 'We could always meet him for dinner.'

'Oh yes, Harry will understand.'

'Nice chap, Harry.'

The menu included such uncertain delights as Prawn Cram Fied, Italian Hotti Potti, Pokhara Scrumbled Edge and Chicken Bomb, but who were we to quibble?

It was John's turn to burst into song. 'Food, glorious food,' he hymned to the astonished waiter, 'cold jelly and custard . . . .'

We emerged two hours later with five rupees between us. Unfortunately the bank was shut. We made what haste we could to the Hungry Eye and found Harry just about to leave. He too, it seemed, had just done himself proud and he waved aside our excuses. Thus encouraged, we asked him if by any chance he was in a position to make us a small loan. Sure; how much did we want? Well, forty rupees would probably see us through until tomorrow, as long as that wasn't going to leave him short. No sir, he could stand us that all right; he was glad to help.

'Nice chap, Harry,' John agreed.

It was, by a nice coincidence, Christmas Eve, but no Santa could have roused us that night even had he brought the chimney down with him (not that there was one).

We opened Bruce's presents at the appropriate time with appropriate ceremony and found them to contain the two halves of his Mars Bar. We were much moved by the sacrifice involved.

As Christians everywhere else were doubtless doing, but with less excuse, we abandoned ourselves to sloth and gluttony.

- 'Full breakfast' in the hotel proved not quite full enough to include fried bread with our fried eggs, and it took several days of careful instruction to an uncomprehending kitchen staff before the omission was repaired. Tea also posed its problems: for reasons which were never obvious to us, bread was served but not toast, and we had to make what we could of the dining room's single and very volatile electric fire. For our main meals we went ever further afield: from the Indira to the Hungry Eye, the Mandarin, Tashi's, the Tibetan Dragon, the Tokyo, the Unity, the Pie'n Chaie. The taste of fresh meat had become such a novelty that it was now a case of 'Buff with everything': Buff Steaks, Buff San, Buff Dal, Buff Pilas, Buff Chow Mein, culminating in Buff Stroganoff at the Yak and Yeti. As for the last, it seemed that, even after booking a table and receiving explicit directions, we were never going to get any nearer this place of legend. We were assured that we were in the right road, but although we went up and down it several times there was no sign of the cosy little bistro that we were looking for. At last someone offered to take us to it in person. He led us through a pair of imposing gateposts and we saw that our mistake had been one of scale: at the end of a long drive stood a sumptuous, colonnaded building which might have been lifted straight out of the Loire Valley. It was extensively floodlit, and the entrance was furnished with a forty-yard carpet and awning. Nor was all this a mere façade: the interior was, if anything, even more splendid. A broad, chandeliered corridor led on one side to a ballroom set about with balconies and lit up at its far end by a multi-coloured Christmas tree reaching almost to its tall ceiling; on the other to a dining-room arranged in intimately curtained alcoves around a central, circular fire heaped with blazing logs. Each table had its own waiter, and every so often Boris himself would make a circuit to ask us if everything was to our satisfaction. Considering that exactly a week earlier we had been at Lobuje eating dehydrated stew in forty degrees of frost, we could be forgiven for thinking that Cinderella's fairy godmother was up to her tricks again.

However, it was no pumpkin coach that arrived to whisk us away, but an ancient, springless Morris Oxford. After a mile of bouncing around in this appalling rattletrap we were uneasily aware that the moment of retribution for all this indulgence was at hand. Sure enough, by the morning we were both dashing in and out of the bathroom like a couple of yoyos. To make matters worse, the plumbing system soon collapsed under this double assault. A team of men presently arrived to dismember it, and for the rest of the day we watched in mounting suspense as they tramped back and forth with various bits and pieces. The outcome of all their labour was an interesting one: the lavatory now flushed with hot water.

Deprived of the pleasures of the body, we sought consolation in more abstract fields. John buried himself in the town's only English-language bookshop, which was having a sale. He returned in a state of considerable excitement with the Penguin Book of Verse of Heaven and Hell in Ancient Mesopotamia; I could have it as soon as he had finished with it himself, he promised. In the meantime I had to make do with the *Times of India* reports on the First Test in Delhi. They were presented in terms of a five-act tragedy.

The first struck a traditional note of foreboding: 'The only certainty about Indian cricket is its glorious uncertainty. We have known moments of joy as well as moments of anguish. And we went through the whole process all over again today as India tottered on the brink of total disaster, but managed to last out the day with a score of 156 for 7.'

The second offered hope that everything might turn out well after all: 'India's batting may be fickle and frail, but the bowling has always been faithful. Shortly after lunch England were past 50 in reply to India's 173 with Wood and Amiss set in their ways. The cool, calculated manner in which they collected their runs suggested an intention to lay the foundation of a massive score;

there was none of that insane flurry of strokes, the slapdash, hell-for-leather attitude which shows in this city's taxi drivers. But the moment Chandrasekhar had dealt the first blow, it was a different story. Bedi's mastery over flight and spin were as good as ever; there may be many claimants to his title, but there is only one Bedi.

The third spoke of folly and error on the grand scale: 'Pace and swing one day, spin and flight another, anything seems too much for our batsmen. The triumph and tragedy of today's play found India in deep trouble. The stellar deed of that baby-faced wonder, Chandrasekhar, who had the career best figures of 8 for 80 in restricting England's score to 200 and their lead to a seemingly inconsequential 27 was almost forgotten before the day ended. Our batsmen, as brittle as Amritsar *papad*, frittered away all the advantage the freak spinner had gained, half the side crumbling for a mere 123.'

The fourth hinted darkly that supernatural forces were at work: 'Oh, what a day! We might as well have been sitting on razor's edge as fortunes tilted tantalizingly this way and that. Old Santa Claus is guarding his secret most zealously, for we still do not have much of a clue as to who will receive his gift packet in the shape of a Test victory. England? Most likely, for they need only 101 for victory and have seven wickets on hand. Did we sight a grim pointer to the result when we saw Venkat of all people floor a simple catch my little daughter could not possibly have missed? And to think of it! Only a little earlier that amazing bundle of energy called Abid Ali made a mess of two catches in the deep, like perhaps never before. It all seemed unbelievable, as though some evil spirit had suddenly descended on us.'

The fifth described the inevitable conclusion: 'England wrapped up their victory by 7 wickets shortly after lunch. Within an hour it was clear that only a miracle could swing the game the other way. Twice Bedi changed ends with Chandra, but the magic would not work; the medium was not made for him. The message was clear: the worst had come to pass.'

The stage seemed set for Shaver Swish.

The problem of my watch began to weigh increasingly on my mind.

On enquiring at the British Embassy I was told that no one had handed it in to claim the reward which I had publicised on the trail.

I went next to the police station (there is only one in Kathmandu) and was led through a labyrinth of mean, concrete cells to the Lost Property Office, which was empty. After waiting half an hour in vain for its occupant to appear, I filled in the appropriate form and left. I called finally at the offices of the *Rising Nepal* to put in an advertisement being careful to describe it as only of 'artificial gold'.

When all these sources drew a blank, I was reduced to going up to anyone in the street I saw wearing a watch and asking him the time, but as everybody in Kathmandu seemed to have a watch I soon realised that this was rather a futile exercise. I could only wait now for the others to return and hope that Jangbu would have some news for me.

The New Year introduced itself in the persons of Bruce and Richard, who had come on a day ahead by sprinting down the last stage to Lamosangu. It was a relief to know from this that they had suffered no lasting effects from their ordeal on the glacier. They spoke of a jolly time being had by all on Christmas Day, but of a steady evaporation of goodwill thereafter, ending with bitter accusations that the porters were eating more than their fair share of potatoes. It was just what John and I had anticipated.

I went to meet the rest when they arrived next day at the Snow View. Jangbu nodded an expressionless greeting, so that it was some minutes before I bothered to ask him about the watch.

'I know the man who has found it.' It was said quite casually.

'You do?'

'Yes. He lives in Petku.'

'How d'you know it's my watch?'

'He showed it to me. He is selling it for seven hundred rupees.'

'Well, I'll see what the police have to say about that. Where is this place?'

'It is about one hour above the first camp.'

'Will you come with me tomorrow to get it? You can have the reward if you do.'

'Yes, I will come.' For the first time there was a note of interest in his voice.

Fabian sensibly declined to lend me the Land-Rover for the day. The travel agencies confirmed that there was a public bus service to Lamosangu, but they could only hazard a guess as to its timetable. At the yard which served for the bus station there was general agreement that the first bus would leave at 6 am and the last return at 4.30 pm; the journey would take at least four hours. It seemed that we might just be able to do it all the same day. Jangbu agreed to meet me at the Panorama at 5.30 the next morning.

I called again at the police station and walked past an indignant corporal into the office of the Deputy Superintendent. A youngish man with a rather bored expression, he showed himself pleased to see me and spoke happily of the six months which he had recently spent at the Hendon Police Training College. He agreed that even under Nepalese law the man had no right to claim any money for my watch except what I cared to give him as a reward and he willingly made out an order to his colleagues at Lamosangu that they were to lend me all possible assistance. I was intrigued to see that there was such a thing as a typewriter in Nepalese script; it was a formidable machine.

I anticipated my alarm clock, but not soon enough to forestall the approach of the night porter singing at the top of his voice.

'You didn't have to tell him to wake the whole building,' I heard John mutter.

Downstairs, several sleeping forms were stretched out on top of the reception desk. One of them pulled down his muffler wound around his face, blinked at me, turned over—and crashed to the floor. Of Jangbu there was no sign.

After waiting twenty minutes for him, I set out for the Sherpa lodge where he had told me he was staying. This was easily traced to a narrow alley in the old quarter, but when roused, the proprietor disclaimed all knowledge of him. I went up and down it shouting his name, but no one stirred except the two old women sweeping the garbage into piles with their besom brooms. In the half light of dawn I counted several dead rats. Knocking up each house in turn soon made me so unpopular that I decided to put the whole thing off for a day and return to the hotel.

Turning into the next street I saw a familiar form fifty yards ahead of me.

'Jangbu!'

'Oh hello, Michael.' It might have been said on the 8.20 from Haywards Heath.

'I thought you said you would meet me at five at the Panorama.'

'Yes, I was just coming.'

'It now happens to be after six and we've missed the bus.'

'There is another one in one hour.'

'Are you sure?'

'Yes, I am sure.'

'There had better be.'

And fortunately for him, there was.

Our fellow-passengers included a herd of goats, half-a-dozen hens trussed up in an old blanket and a tinker who filled the entire back row with two sackfuls of empty oil cans. He also had with him a bottle of *rakshi*, to which he helped himself at regular intervals, eventually coming to blows with the conductor who tried to take it away from him. The hens left us in no doubt of their resentment, and one of them made such effective use of a brief spell of liberty that the driver refused to continue until it had been recaptured. Much the best behaved were the goats, who stood throughout the journey in the aisle browsing contentedly on occasional offerings of tangerine skin.

Under these conditions it was perhaps no occasion for surprise that it should take us four hours to cover fifty miles.

The sergeant at the police station was much impressed by his superior's note and lost no time in detailing two men to accompany me. They both looked superbly fit, nor did they show any resentment at being lumbered with such a job. Jangbu had meanwhile disappeared into one of the many curry stalls for his lunch and half an hour passed before he could be traced. It was thus almost noon before we started, which meant that we had to cover the ground twice as fast as we had done a month earlier. Without the twin handicap of pack and boots, I supposed that it might be just possible.

The two policemen set off at a pace which indicated that they at least were going to make it. I was soon left struggling in their wake, having at the same time coax Jangbu along, who had either over-eaten himself or given up all prospect of the reward. However, we reached the first teahouse, which I remembered as being roughly half way to the camp site, just on the hour. I called a brief halt.

A bizarre figure rose to greet us from the side of the path. He wore sunglasses, winkle-picker shoes, a rather flashy blue suit and a tie which elsewhere might have been taken as an Old Wykhamist's; fifteen years earlier he would have looked quite the part in the King's Road. He offered me a peanut in passable English, introduced himself as a Radio Nepal 'student technician' on a visit to his family in the village above Petku and asked me the purpose of my journey. Not being at all sure that I wanted him to know, I made some vague answer about trekking, and was consequently rather galled to learn a few minutes later that the policemen had told him everything. I ordered them to move off again immediately in the hope of throwing him off, but he stuck to us like a leech all the way.

When we got to the village Jangbu pointed out the house, which was a little below the main path. The plan was that the policemen should lie in wait round the next corner while Jangbu introduced me as a prospective buyer; I would then ask to see the watch, grab it and if there was any trouble, call them up with the whistle.

It didn't quite work out like that.

The house was empty when we arrived, and we returned to confer with the others (Winkle-pickers still refused to leave us alone). As they emerged from their hiding place, the man appeared. He was quite the shiftiest character I had ever seen, studying us with mean, foxy eyes behind an inane grin. The sight of the policemen was enough to make him deny at first that he'd ever had the watch, then that he still had it, having sold it three weeks ago to a friend who had taken it to Kathmandu and sold it there. Everyone seemed quite content to accept this statement, and it was only after strenuous prompting that I got Jangbu to confront him with the fact that two days earlier he had been offering it for sale. He then went into a huddle with the policemen, at the end of which he was reported as saying that it had once been in his possession but that it was now in the next village with the man who had jointly bought it with him off the child who had originally found it, that they were demanding eight hundred rupees for it and that anyway he wasn't going anywhere until he'd had his lunch.

As we waited for him, the policemen told me via Winkle-pickers that I must expect to part with that sum. Jangbu by now seemed to have abdicated all responsibility in the matter.

Our quarry reappeared at two o'clock and led us up to the next village with an insolent swagger. His partner in crime was traced to the teahouse. By the time developments had been explained to him we were surrounded by the entire population for miles around. In desperation I pointed out that it was now three o'clock but to no effect, and we moved off once more to, I assumed, yet another village. After a hundred yards, however, a sheet of tissue paper was suddenly produced and my watch unwrapped from it. I asked to see if it was intact, but there was no question now of making a grab and dashing off with it. Winkle-pickers took over the negotiations and presently announced that he had beaten them down to six hundred. Only wanting to be rid of the whole squalid business, I raised no objection—even when he kept a hundred for himself and vanished over the horizon with it. The watch was mine again, that was all that mattered.

Impelled more by our weight than anything else, we made the return journey in an hour and a quarter compared with the three it had taken us in the morning and the six on the original trek. We could hear the bus hooting as we limped over the bridge into Lamosangu, and it was already on the move when we reached the road. We ran behind it shouting and waving our arms, and after a hundred yards it condescended to stop.

The tinker was still on the back seat; the oil cans had been replaced by another bottle of *rakshi*.

Presently he noticed my watch and leant across to tap it.

'What is time?' he leered.

What indeed? Perhaps only in Nepal did the question have such deep philosophical significance.

He offered me a swig, which I accepted. After all, I had reason to celebrate: a wallet in Persia, a passport in India, a watch in Nepal. What odds, I wondered, would Ladbroke's have given against such a treble?

17 ROMANTIC ENDING

As we passed through the market place on our departure from
Kathmandu a small boy ran out into the road causing Fabian to
swerve violently. We looked back to see that a pile of tangerines
had been neatly bisected. The boy (who was slightly grazed) cost us
ten rupees in compensation, the tangerines fifteen. It was the
nearest we had come to an event of interest in our three weeks in
the place.

Before we left, Jangbu told me something which made me think
that I had judged him rather harshly: he was only eighteen. At any
rate, we parted the best of friends. He presented me with a
handsome Tibetan woodcut, and I topped up his reward with my
boots which he seemed to think he could get a good price for. I
have to admit to some moments of sadistic pleasure at the thought
that some poor innocent may even today be hobbling about the
Himalayas in them.

John came away with his profit and loss account roughly in
balance. On the debit side the dry cleaners had failed to return his
trousers in time; on the other he had dug out of a metalwork shop
a fantastical creation which was optimistically described as a 'wine
jar' (as far as I had been able to discover, there was no wine to be
had in Kathmandu). Later, however, it was found both to leak and
to give him lead poisoning.

Long stretches of the road to Pokhara were still under
construction. Lines of workmen sat patiently breaking up stones
with hammers into gravel which others then loaded into baskets
and scattered over the surface, treading them in with their bare
feet; tar was then sprayed on it from an oil barrel on wheels
equipped with a hand-operated pump. The Chinese overseers
were easily distinguished by their wide-brimmed straw hats; one
was seen quoting aloud from his Little Red Book, to the tolerant

amusement of the natives. They might not have been so amused if they had been better acquainted with the consequences that Chinese road-building had brought to Tibet.

We camped overnight just outside the town beside a lake. The views of Dhaulagiri and Annapurna were very fine; the rice pudding at the Prince Hotel hardly less so.

The road to the border had fortunately been completed, making an easy day's run. The chirping of cicadas and, less inviting, the whining of mosquitoes, announced our return to the Indian border. Fabian considered that we would be safe enough from their attentions on the verandah of a dak bungalow; John and I thought otherwise and took a room in a modest hotel round the corner. The wisdom of our decision was soon confirmed by the arrival of a waiter with a large flitgun.

In the morning I joined a disorderly queue at the bank to exchange our remaining Nepalese rupees. Through a hole in the grille no more than four fingers wide I had some difficulty in following the clerk's calculations, which were made in Nepali script on the back of an envelope. Returning to the relative calm of the Land-Rover, I found that I was some seventy (Indian) rupees short. I went back with little hope of recovering them, but he retrieved the envelope from the floor, re-checked the figures and cheerfully corrected his mistake.

That was Nepal all over.

Three days of dodging bicycles, bullock-carts and drunk-driven lorries brought us to the Corbett National Game Park, described by the guidebook as 'show piece of Indian wild life'. Memories of the Apollo Circus, however, led us not to expect too much.

The admission charge was fifteen rupees, but for students two. Only Bruce had the appropriate card, but in the gathering dusk four of us were able to pass ourselves off on it before the suspicions of the myopic janitor were aroused. The 'residential area'—four marquees and a wash-house—'lay in the heart of the jungle' twenty miles up a rutted track; the eggs intended for supper were already well scrambled when we reached it.

No one complained in the night of being disturbed by prowling wildlife.

The afternoon was set aside for a 'tiger hunt', although this depended on some co-operation on the part of the tigers: a bait would be laid and the rest would be up to them. We were free to use the morning to rout out as many other exciting beasts as we could find.

We bounced down an even rougher track to the crocodile pool and for an hour waited in vain for something to break the surface; we toured the jungle and glimpsed a couple of monkeys in the branches fifty feet above our heads; we climbed up to an observation post to survey the elephant grass and saw only a small herd of unremarkable deer—but then the tigers were going to make up for all that, we told ourselves.

Two elephants had been reserved for us out of the five that made up the taxi fleet. The news that one of them had suddenly been taken out of service caused momentary consternation, but we were assured that there would still be enough room on the other four if we squashed up—we would just have to hold on a bit tighter, that was all.

The rest of the party arrived in a trio of Cadillacs. In a country where, thanks to an import ban on foreign cars, everyone has to muddle along in locally produced Morris Oxfords, this marked them as Very Important People Indeed. We asked the head warden who they might be, and he replied in tones of reverence that they were film stars. The ones that stared so monotonously at us from all those lurid posters which plastered every major town? No, not as important as *that*—we could hardly expect to meet *them*—but stars nonetheless, and he went on to remind us that the Indian film industry was now the largest in the world (a fact which should not surprise, given a population of five hundred million and not a single television set between them). They gave themselves airs to match, making no attempts to hide their displeasure at having to 'squash up' with us.

Presently the elephants appeared in line ahead and knelt obediently for us to mount.

The hunt was on.

> We jumped aboard and clung
> To the overcrowded howdah,
> Hoping someone had a gun
> And a modicum of powder
>
> In case a crowd of tigers

Thought of adding to their dinner;
We checked our life insurance
And wished ourselves in Pinner.

Then the beasts began to lurch
Along the jungle trail,
Through bog and brush and palm
Where the nuts were not for sale.

And we peered about like sparrows
For the slightest signs of life
For tiger, tiger burning bright
And his more voracious wife.

And just to entertain us
Our mahout said 'Drop some gear',
So we did, and it was picked up
By a grey trunk at the rear

And handed back politely
Without even breaking stride,
For elephants—we know—
Are as suave as they are wide.

Then we forged across a river
With still nothing but the birds
And the elephants, who splashed us
With their massive, shot-putt turds.

We strode on through the long grass
Till we came into a clearing
Where we climbed onto some platforms
And strained our eyes and hearing.

We stood with bated breath up there
With cameras at the ready
While the tigers chewed a donkey-leg—
We felt sorry for the neddy.

But this was quite invisible

Being hidden in the grass;
There was silence, heavy breathing
And the flash of Nippon glass.

Then we heard a horrid growl
As the beaters closed the trap
And out a tiger lolloped
Across the narrow gap.

Now he was not tremendous—
But a real tiger was he—
And he was shortly followed
By the other one—his she.

And she went bounding over
As fast as she could run;
In fact both tigers came and went
Like the firing of a gun.

Some clicked their cameras far too late
And some cried out in rage—
For a well-trained tiger should be slow,
Like his brothers in a cage.

Two seconds flat we'd seen him for,
One and a half the lady,
And in view of what we'd paid
We thought it rather shady.

For we had travelled many leagues
To see this awesome sight—
A real live tiger roaming loose
Complete with roar and bite.

We shall return the sadder
To Clapham, Leeds and Oban,
And in years to come we shall instead
Go down to Bath and Woburn.

Our bill included the following item: Tiger charges, 60 rupees.

Someone calculated that that gave them an earnings rate of rather over £10,000 an hour.

If the four 'students' had felt any remorse before, they suffered none now.

We stayed in Delhi just long enough to catch the result of the Second Test played in Calcutta.

It was not merely on the front page of the *Times of India:* it was the front page. 'India wrought a miracle here today.' Ran the opening sentence. 'They won the second Test against England by 28 runs. And for long hours thereafter Eden Gardens and its environs were virtually transformed into the Garden of Eden. . . .'

The same edition carried the following report of the National Athletics Championships: 'India's representative at the Commonwealth Games at Edinburgh, T.Y.Biredar of Mysore, won the marathon in a time of 2 hours, 53 minutes, 10 seconds here today. A ticket collector with the Southern Railway, he raced into the stadium for the final lap well past noon. The scorching heat had prevented him giving of his best. On four occasions he had to break his rhythm and walk. As he trudged on wearily, the sporting crowd cheered warmly. Up to the 19th mile T.Eshwar of Mysore was second, but at that stage he was forced to retire because of acute cramps and taken to hospital. Haryana policeman Tek Chand quickened his pace and finished second in 13 hours, 4 minutes, 41 seconds. . . .'

After that it was no surprise to read that in winning the 80 metres hurdles Chandra Padhi 'crept into the limelight'.

We learnt that Indo-Pakistani suspicions of each other had now declined sufficiently to allow the border to open two days a week instead of only one as formerly, and our crossing of it was duly reduced from eight hours to four.

At Lahore we parted from our original route to make the long sweep southward which would take us through Baluchistan and Southern Persia on John's promised pilgrimage to Shiraz (it has to be said that the prospect of seeing Persepolis also had something to do with the rest of us acceding to this pledge). From there he had worked out a still more ambitious diversion to Baghdad, undeterred by the intermittent warfare being waged on the Iraqi-Persian border. Another obstacle defeated him, however: in order to obtain the necessary visa he had to provide evidence of the absence of Jewish blood in his veins, and in this he was no more successful than he had been in his attempt to prove to the Yugoslavs that he was not a Ugandan Asian.

I too suffered a disappointment, although hardly on the same scale. The first significant town after Lahore was marked on the map as Montgomery, but was found to have been renamed Sahiwal. I had my revenge, however; as we emerged from it a bicyclist fell in behind us pedalling furiously to take advantage of the slipstream—until we had to brake hard for an oncoming lorry; he sensibly preferred the nearest tree to the back of the trailer. Greatly to its credit, the local biscuit factory had stood out against such prosaic tendencies, and Montgomery's Lemon Creams were to accompany us all the way to the Persian border.

We crossed the Indus basin on pontoons supported by barges whose woodwork had been bleached white by long exposure to the sun; it was difficult to envisage the transformation of these sluggish streams into the raging torrents that were to wreak such destruction only a few months later.

On its other side we climbed into a gorge which lifted us four thousand feet to the Baluchi plateau. Over a thousand miles in length, it was even more of a wilderness than the country's northern neighbour, Afghanistan. We were not surprised to read later of secessionist movements in the area, for its fierce-featured inhabitants bore little resemblance to their more effete fellow-countrymen of the plain. As if to compensate for their desolation they had endowed their towns with some delightful names: Tump, Wad, Pip, Bent, Qir, Baft, Bam, Boluk, Turbat, Rish Pish. Mr Jingle would have felt at home.

The rise in altitude brought our interlude of warmth to an abrupt end.

Stopping at Quetta to pick up our Persian visas, we found the consulate shut for the day. The Hotel Lourdes was reported to be the best available but at seventy rupees for a room largely taken up by a vast, primeval boiler—we would have to pay another ten to light it—we decided that it was strictly for the faithful (whoever they might be) and settled instead for the no more modest Farah at quarter the price. We dined there on the unlikely combination of Châteaubriand Steak and Ruby Port; they both pleasantly surprised, although nobody was prepared to speculate on the origin of either. The rest of the evening was spent in the English-speaking cinema, with less happy results: the main film was a hunter-and-his-woman-in-the-Rockies-in-midwinter yarn of such surpassing gaucherie that it soon had the locals (unaided by any subtitles) rolling in the aisles.

A single-track railway now accompanied us all the way to the Persian border. In three days we saw no train—no doubt a sensible economy, for it was not at all clear who should ever want to use such a line. The desert took on a billiard-table flatness, provoking a long argument as to whether the extensive lake which now appeared on our right was merely a mirage; a change in the angle of vision caused by a dip in the road eventually proved it to be so. The sight of a gang of workmen on the railway led me to think that I had again been similarly deceived. As I approached with my camera to record the phenomenon, they suddenly ran towards me and formed up in a straight line, picks and shovels at the slope. Nothing could persuade them to resume their work, and they were still rigidly at attention when we drove off again.

Our first night in Persia was marked by a sandstorm, which blew away one of the tents. It was only retrieved after prolonged pursuit.

Other mishaps followed: a shattered windscreen, the loss of half the map to a goat who had apparently mistaken its orange cover for a tangerine skin, and after a night at seven thousand feet a frozen radiator (the garage in Kathmandu had evidently omitted to replace the anti-freeze). To make up for the time lost we now had to take the most direct route to Shiraz, which the remnants of the map indicated as lying through Sirjan and over the bed of a salt lake. Some doubted its viability, but it was confidently classed as a main road and when we reached it, the crust seemed firm enough. Within two hundred yards the Land-Rover was axle-deep in treacly mud.

Heaving and pushing until our spattered clothes looked like so many suits of leopard skin, we were just able to free it. For another two hundred yards it made reasonable progress, then sank again. By mid-afternoon it was clear even to John that it must eventually founder with all hands if we continued, and Fabian turned back. On the way we passed a lorry which had done just that; its driver pleaded with us to try and pull him out, but he didn't take offence when we declined. He told us of another route further north, but a check at the police station ruled out that too as 'finished'.

Even Persepolis was now in jeopardy; the best alternative route involved a diversion of at least two hundred miles, and that was described by Fabian's AA notes as 'rough gravel'. Fortunately they proved out of date and a spanking new highway saw us there with an afternoon to spare.

'I don't know why we have to stop for this useless pile when Shiraz is only another fifty miles,' John lamented, but he found no supporters.

In truth the major excavations currently in progress detracted somewhat from the grandeur of the site: the scaffolding that encased several of the columns gave it something of the appearance of an oil refinery. Nor did it hold a great deal for the layman—some fine but monotonous friezes of loyal subjects doing homage to the great King, a few striking heads of horses and lions rampant, the incised signature of Stanley (but not Byron).

We consoled ourselves that this was more than Herat, Kandahar and Kabul had had to offer between them on the northern route.

It was snowing when we got to Teheran.

Remembering Fabian's warning of the worse horrors that lay ahead, I began to consider other possible means of transport. John had spoken of a friend who had taken a train from Istanbul to, he thought, Teheran, but when pressed he wasn't prepared to swear to it and there was an ominous hiatus in the map's railway system across the sixty miles of Lake Van just the other side of the Turkish border. At the station, however, I learnt all, or nearly all, that I could wish to hear. There was indeed such a service: it ran once a week and as it happened, the next train was leaving at nine o'clock the very next morning, arriving in Istanbul three days later. All the sleepers had already been booked and I would have to wait until the morning to obtain a second class ticket.

I asked John if he was interested in coming with me, but the weight of his disappointment was still such as to prevent him from reaching any decision. Instead, he talked vaguely of joining me on a boat to Athens when we met up again in Istanbul.

Waking early—too early for farewells, which was perhaps just as well in view of the resentment expressed in some quarters that I alone should have enough money to be able to consider alternatives—from an uneasy night of suspense, I arrived at the station well before seven, only to find that a considerable queue had preceded me. To increase my anxiety still further the clerk took upon himself most of the duties of an immigration official, demanding to see everyone's visas, passports and vaccination certificates. It was another hour before I had the precious ticket in my hand. I noticed from the booking plan that there were only three or four seats left apart from one whole compartment left mysteriously empty. My request to be transferred to it was peremptorily refused.

My immediate fellow-passengers turned out to be seven Pakistanis, who seemed to have brought everything except the proverbial kitchen sink with them. They were models of politeness and courtesy, but however they rearranged their possessions no space could be found for me. In the end I told them not to bother and went in search of the ticket collector to find out if there had been any sleeper cancellations. There hadn't been.

As I returned down the platform a head leant out of a window and said: 'You English?'

'Yes.'

'Would you like to sit with me? I have this compartment for myself.'

'Very much in that case. But won't there be some other people coming?'

' No, only the second driver at Tabriz and he will go again at the border. I have arranged it.'

'How? I tried to but they told me I couldn't.'

'Perhaps you did not give them enough baksheesh. Go to get your luggage and I will wait for you.'

The Pakistanis were as relieved as I was by my departure.

My new friend introduced himself as Sohrab. Tall and sleek, he wore a smart blazer and dark polo-necked sweater. He was on his way to Ankara University, having previously spent a year at a language school in Cambridge. His father was one of the Shah's generals, but he himself hoped to go into the Diplomatic Corps.

'In Turkey the trains are not so good as this,' he told me, 'so enjoy yourself while you can.'

With the snow piling up deeper and deeper outside, that was not difficult.

At Tabriz twelve hours later we were duly joined by the relief driver and his stoker. They made no complaint at finding us, and for the most part sat in awed silence, regarding Sohrab as more of a stranger than me. They got out at the next stop to take over the engine and we settled down for a comfortable night's sleep, only briefly disturbed by the two parties of passport inspectors.

We reached Lake Van shortly after noon the next day in bright sunshine. There was scarcely a ripple on its waters to disturb the dazzling reflections of the surrounding mountains. Only the first-class carriages went aboard the ferry, which might have passed as a British Rail Cross-Channel steamer; its bill of fare—cheese rolls, chocolate and Coke—supported such a comparison. According to Sohrab his country had provided the money for it.

Half way across the sky clouded over and we arrived at the other side in gathering gloom. It was a shock to emerge from the warmth of the saloon into the bitter cold, and still more of one to realise that there was no train to greet us. Sohrab and I took refuge in the corridor of one of the carriages until a ticket collector arrived and ordered us off. He was a great brute of a man and would clearly have thought nothing of throwing us down the six feet to the steel deck; Sohrab's proferred baksheesh was knocked aside and we beat a hasty retreat to the open stern.

Presently an engine arrived, but only to take off the carriages. After a similar interval a line of goods wagons were shunted aboard in their place, but there was still no sign of any other carriages. The cold was now intolerable and we rejoined the rest of the passengers in the saloon.

Another hour passed before the lights of the engine were seen approaching once more, provoking a general rush to the gangway. The nightmare of Muzaffarpur was re-enacted all over again, this time in three feet of snow and thirty degrees of frost. Losing contact with Sohrab in the melee, I scrambled inside the leading carriage, only to be told that it was going on to the ferry. I jumped off again into the snow, struggled on to the next one—to find it packed full of stolid, cloth-capped Turks. The next was exactly the same. The one after that was first class, but the sight of an empty seat was too much for me and I claimed it. The ticket collector then reappeared and threatened to throw me off again, refusing to listen to my offer to pay the difference. The confusion in the corridor was now even worse because word had got round that some of the carriages weren't going as far as Istanbul. Behind, the sharp edge of a tin trunk banged against my shins; in front, the ferrule of an umbrella jabbed into my ribs. I found another seat, second class this time, but the other occupants of the compartment refused to let me in and a comical exchange of fisticuffs ensued through a six-inch gap in the door. I fought on through another two carriages and came at last to a compartment only half filled. I forced my way into it before any resistance could be organised and seized a corner. I was lectured, abused, reviled, pinched, poked, and pummelled, but nothing was going to move me; there I remained sitting upright for the rest of the night. Two soldiers entered and sat beside me, confirming my opinion of the rifle as an unsatisfactory bedfellow.

At eight the next morning I felt sufficiently confident that my presence was accepted to go in search of the restaurant car, and to my great surprise found a meal recognisable as breakfast in full swing. Sohrab was already on his third cup of coffee; having spent the night on a trunk in the corridor, he had lost some of his suavity.

'Stupid, bloody people,' he fulminated. 'We give them a ship, we build them a railway and they cannot even run a train properly.'

I spent the rest of the day there with him in this relative haven. Outside, the snow gradually receded from the hills, but the train gathered no pace in its descent, stopping at every smallest halt and not a few times in open country. He reckoned that it was already seven hours behind schedule and being due in at Ankara at midnight he resigned himself to another sleepless night.

Returning after the last dinner to the compartment, I made another pleasant discovery: the soldiers had departed, leaving me to share one side with the middle-aged man who had been my chief persecutor the previous evening. He had already stretched himself out on the inside, and when I lay down on the outside he made a point of thrusting his feet in my face. By stages I was able to work them away and under my armpit, but in retaliation he promptly knocked my feet off the window table where they rested. This futile war of attrition went on all night until six in the morning when one of the others gave up his place in the luggage rack to me. I thus missed Sohrab's departure.

We finally drew into Istanbul's Asian terminal at nine o'clock that evening, thirteen hours late. It was with some wry amusement that a week after my return to England I heard a railway enthusiast express his opinion on the wireless that this was 'the most romantic train journey in the world today'.

None of the taxi drivers that met the ferry at the Galata Bridge knew of the hotel that Sohrab had recommended to me. I ordered the most persistent of them to take me to any modern, central hotel and, too tired to argue, accepted his quoted price of 'fifty'.

Two minutes later he pulled up outside a couple of quite promising possibilities standing almost side by side. I paid him his fifty kurus and made for the nearest of them, only to be yanked back by the sleeve.

'What's the matter?'

'You give me fity kurus.'

'Well, that's what we agreed.'

'No, fifty lira.'

'Don't be absurd. That's nearly two pounds.'

'I say fifty lira, you say fifty lira, then we go.'

'I meant kurus.'

'Lira.'

'Kurus!'

And so it went on. Eventually I conceded that the equivalent of tuppence was rather mean even if we had gone no more than a quarter of a mile and split the difference in decimals at five lira. He was still not satisfied, however, and tugged at my coat all the way to the reception desk of the Hotel Dilson.

They had one room left, the receptionist told me. It was all that I could desire: clean, warm, quiet and with a bath, but at 120 lira it occurred to me that I might be able to find the same for less in the Hotel Keban. I told her to keep it provisionally for me and went next door. They too only had one room left which was cheaper but inferior, and I decided that after what I'd been through on the train I deserved nothing but the best for one night at least—to find that the room at the Dilson had been let in my absence. The taxi driver had disappeared, leaving me to draw the obvious conclusion.

I returned wearily to the Keban and asked to be allowed to test the hot water before committing myself. Of course it was hot, the manager told me indignantly, but if I didn't like his hotel, then I could go elsewhere.

'All right, all right,' I said, 'I'll take it'.

His pledge was fulfilled, and all my fatigue and frustration soon ebbed away through willing pores. It would be some time before I went again without my nightly bath, I decided; John was welcome to the Aegean, but I was going home.

I picked up a BEA timetable on my way down to breakfast the next morning.

There was only one other person in the dining room, a tall girl with long blonde hair. I smiled tentatively and made the excuse of ordering an elaborate breakfast at the bar in order to give her a chance to respond. It worked, for as I made for a table in her direction she had a question ready for me. I answered it and asked if I might join her. Yes, of course I could; it was nice to have someone to talk to. She was Australian and on her way home from a skiing tour of America and Europe. Her flight was 4.20 that afternoon; when was mine? I turned to the timetable to find out; it was 4.25. That looked after that one. She had to leave me now because she had booked on a morning's bus tour of the city; perhaps we could meet for lunch. . . .

Later, I wandered over the Galata Bridge and up the other side for another look at the Topkapi. As I studied my guidebook just inside the entrance a voice said 'Hello'; I looked up and found my new friend beside me. It was beginning to seem almost more than a coincidence.

We lunched, packed and took a taxi together to the airport. Our two flights were called simultaneously and we kissed a hurried farewell at the barrier.

I had not dreamt of such an ending to these past four months.

EPILOGUE

The others got back a fortnight later minus, of course, John. He had stopped off at Ankara to have a look at the Hittite museum, but had caught them up again in Istanbul where they had left him talking of taking a boat not to Athens, but Marseilles. The journey had been every bit as cold as Fabian had predicted: on their first night in Turkey the radiator had again frozen up even though it had been replenished with anti-freeze. To try them still further, the Land-Rover had begun to fall to bits on the return through Europe; two days had been lost in Germany while a new half shaft was obtained.

In short, they were glad to be back.

Another month passed without any further word of John. It was suggested that shipping in the Eastern Mediterranean should be alerted to look out for a large buffalo horn.

Then out of the blue a letter arrived from Beirut in his inimitable scrawl, saying that he was flying home the next day.

When we met for a drink at the Rosslyn Arms, he did not immediately volunteer any explanation of his absence.

'I thought you were meant to be heading for Marseilles.'

'Yes, I was.'

'But Beirut's not exactly in the same direction.'

'No. You see I was all lined up to get on this boat to Tunis—'

'Tunis?'

'—which went on to Palermo and Marseilles, when the dollar crisis struck and by the time I got my travellers' cheques changed the boat had gone.'

'So then?'

'I took a bus to Athens to see if I could get another one there and I bumped into this rather attractive Irish girl in the hotel there.

The only trouble was she was a bit lumbered with this American and the only way I could get her away from him was to tell her what a marvellous place Istanbul was and persuade her to go back there with me.'

'And you succeeded?'

'Well, yes and no. She came with me all right, but as soon as she got there she hopped off with this other American, which was rather annoying.'

'It must have been. So you then persuaded her to come to Beirut with you?'

'No, she had nothing to do with my going there.'

'What did, then?'

'Well, I reckoned if I could get a job there I'd really be able to button up my Arabic, which I've always wanted to do. It's such a bind not being able to read Hafez and Saadi in the original, you see.'

'Yes, John, I see; I see . . .'

As it grows dark
The streets round the grand bazaar
Grow quiet and the merchants and traders
Gather in the cafés and restaurants
To eat and drink, or to listen to the storyteller
Filling out the lineaments of a familiar tale
With strange peoples and voyages.
I make my way past the pale and shadowy majesty
Of the Ayia Sofiya for the last time
And go down the curving street towards the ferry.
Soon, we swing out into the busy waters
And the old city of Sultan Ahmet fades
To form a winking constellation
Behind the timeless Byzantine walls.
A stranger's hand helps me up into the coach
And it glides away; another city
Falls into the night
Beyond us Ankara and the plain veiled with snow,
Then Iskenderum between the sea and mountains
And through Syria to the Levant: all this a tapestry
Of bright and fading memories. . .
So many nights and days . . . so many cities.